Relativism and the Natural Left

RELATIVISM
AND THE
NATURAL LEFT

William P. Kreml

New York University Press • New York *and* London
1984

Copyright © 1984 by New York University
All rights reserved
Manufactured in the United States of America

Library of Congress Cataloging in Publication Data
Kreml, William P.
Relativism and the natural left.
Includes index.
1. Political science.   2. Political psychology.
3. Relativity.   I. Title.
JA74.5.K73 1983   320'.01'9   83-19437
ISBN 0-8147-4584-9
ISBN 0-8147-4585-7 (pbk.)

*Clothbound editions of New York University Press books are Smyth-sewn
and printed on permanent and durable acid-free paper.*

To Liz and Suzie

Acknowledgments

My deep thanks to a number of people who read this manuscript and made useful comments. In particular, I would like to thank Natalie Hevener, Morse Peckham, Peter Sederberg, Philip Zeltner, Daniel Sabia, James Cochrane, and Alfred Mauet. I also would like to thank my graduate assistant, Richard Gleissner. Without all of their help, a challenging piece would have been all the more difficult.

I would also like to thank Dr. James A. Kuhlman and the James F. Byrnes International Center and Dr. Charles W. Kegley, Jr., and the Department of Government and International Studies, University of South Carolina, for their assistance in the publication of this work.

Contents

Introduction	*xiii*
ONE THE CASE FOR REASON	*1*
TWO THE PSYCHOLOGY OF THE THEORY	*49*
THREE THE SOCIAL SCIENCES	*83*
FOUR POLITICS	*143*
FIVE AN EMERGING PHILOSOPHY OF POLITICS	*161*
Index	*177*

The human being, in his profound reality as well as in his great tension of becoming is a divided being, a being which divides again, having permitted himself the illusion of unity for barely an instant.

Gaston Bachelard

Introduction

This work will describe an emergent political philosophy that is based upon a relativistic understanding of human psychology. At one time, the question of human nature was at the center of all political philosophy, even if it was not addressed in relativistic terms. Now much of contemporary philosophy avoids the human nature question altogether, and for the past two hundred years economically based models of political philosophy have provided the core of political thought. Yet even the classical singular perspective theories, along with the revived notions of human nature found in some modern work, have still not tapped the richness of human relativity. The weaknesses of both economic explanations and singular psychological explanations must now give way to a broader understanding of politics, for the very issue of political equity, which is more clearly understood within a relativistic context, is the key to a more robust philosophy of politics.

The essence of a philosophical relativism within politics is not only that there are wholly different qualities of contributions to a political system but that the economic model and its focus upon economic contribution was in fact a representation of a nonrelativistic psychological perspective all along. Ironically, the misplaced reverence that such a model received was in great part due to the confidence of those political interests which felt that the economic model would work well for them. It may have done something for them at one time, but what it is doing now is restricting the scope of the entire debate over political contribution and equity.

Aristotle, among others, had a sense of the inadequacy of an economic framework; what he said in the *Politics* was that "claims to political rights must be based on the ground of contribution to the elements which constitute the being of a state." Why the industrializing societies of recent history were seduced into believing that those elements were solely economic may be understandable, yet we have now come far enough to repudiate any model that contains only a single standard for either human contribution or the human perception of that contribution. The way to enlarge the contributive paradigm is through an understanding of a relativist psychology, the burden of which is that the range of human psychologies is what accounts for the very variety of evaluative equities.

Relativism, in short, asks for a variant standard of judgment, just as it permits a variant notion of political contribution and encourages the recognition of the differences among human natures themselves. An exploration of such differentiations is the burden of *Relativism and the Natural Left*. The way that different contributions are valued, and the search for the origin of differentiated contribution, is what we are about. All and all, it is an argument for a new way of determining political equity, a way that finds itself in new understandings of psychological relativism and an emerging political philosophy.

CHAPTER ONE

The Case for Reason

Objective and Subjective

In Aristotle's *Politics,* there is a discussion that prescribes how the Greeks were supposed to feel about the *méson,* or the mean or center as we would know it today. Aristotle not only argued that "in the ownership of all gifts of fortune" were the Greeks to aim for the middle condition; he also cautioned his fellow citizens to be wary of the "over-handsome, the over-strong, the over-noble [and] the over-wealthy."[1] Appropriately, the other extreme condition was also considered to be undesirable, the "poor," the "weak," and the "ignoble" being perceived as equally distant from the mean and therefore equally objectionable. The conventional reading of this section of the *Politics* is that Aristotle was speaking of gradations of rank or, at the least, of gradations of human qualities. Such qualities are largely objective, and they, again, include the possession of a greater or lesser quantity of various attributes. Though this may be an accurate reading of Aristotle as far as it goes, I am increasingly convinced that these objective or quantitative factors were not of principal importance to Aristotle.

On the contrary, I feel that Aristotle was very aware of the differing attitudes of different people, and I think that he was particularly aware of people's unique preference for one commodity or quality over another. He was, I believe, also dealing with a more subjective kind of human evaluation, that is, he was also concerned with how people thought about the very importance of station and rank itself or how important such things were to different people.

To personally covet an excess of wealth or to feign nobility or to wish to possess more than a reasonable amount of any of these qualities would have signaled the existence of an intemperate subjective state of mind, a condition that Aristotle disapproved of as vigorously as he disapproved of the more objective possession or nonpossession of these qualities themselves. Aristotle's own language reveals the importance of that subjectivity to him when, in that same section of the *Politics,* he contrasts the abhorrent behaviors that lead to violence and serious crime on the one hand with the human tendencies toward "roguery" or "petty offenses" on the other. In this discussion, each of the various sets of behavior may, at first impression, be at the same respective ends of the "vertical" or quantitative continuum as that of Aristotle's objective criteria of wealth, handsomeness, and so forth. In fact, however, I suggest that they portray something that is really more a part of a subjective psychological or qualitative continuum.

This subjective differentiation in the quality of need for the objective ranking itself is perhaps best expressed as a kind of "horizontalism." Just as Aristotle warned against the subjective state of either enjoying or coveting too many advantages, he also warned against a subjective state—so relevant for politics, incidentally—of knowing only how to obey or how to rule but never both.

This latter dichotomy, the propensity for only leading or following, involves, again, a quality of subjectivity, that is, a quality that is not principally related to an objective or "vertical" continuum. The propensity for leadership, in short, is deeply related to the psychological subjectivity of a person's relation to political authority as well as to the demands of an active polity for a particular kind of political leadership. Aristotle felt strongly about this kind of subjectivity because he felt not only that an excessive verticalism within a polity itself but also an excessive subjective affinity for verticalism could bring about what he called a political state of "slaves and masters." That condition itself encourages neither a spirit of friendship nor an improvement of "the temper of a political community."[2] Therefore, the horizontal range within a polity, that is, the subjective range of those who are more or less concerned with objective materialities, would be an important thing to know about any political community.

THE CASE FOR REASON

From Subjectivity to Reason

If there is, then, a second level to Aristotle's thinking beyond the level of vertical gradations, and if we understand the essentially horizontal nature or the subjectivism of that second level, we might then speculate upon the direction of these subjective factors as they played themselves out within Aristotle's thinking. We can locate these factors, I believe, within the context of what Aristotle said about the quality of reason, and the passages that would demonstrate this in Aristotle, again, directly follow those which we have already examined. What was it, after all, that Aristotle found so intolerable about those citizens who coveted excessive wealth and other objective attributes? Or, as he thought of it within the context of politics, what was it that more certainly left some citizens with only the ability to obey or only the ability to rule? He told us, in part, when he said that such people would "find it hard to follow the lead of reason."[3]

The quality of reason, or the quality of living within the dictates of the orders of the universe, is really a kind of third level for Aristotle. It is a higher level of understanding for him, building upon both the objective vertical conditions of life and, perhaps even more directly, upon the subjective, horizontally differentiated way that people think about that condition. Ultimately, Aristotle argued that human reason was affected by covetousness, and as Aristotle was clearly concerned with the question of finding which citizens would have the qualities of reason within them and thus would be able to perceive the principles of fair evaluation of contribution and distribution, those very questions would also be affected by human reason.

The Left and Reason

Relativism and the Natural Left begins with two assumptions. One is that for all political societies, as well as for the one human society, some notion of reason, or even some notion of human equity or justice, is still the primary guidepost for the determination of what normative political philosophy is all about. The second and somewhat more tenuous assumption is that there is a place, a location, or perhaps it might be better to say a collection of locations, that demark the best perspective on what we understand political justice, or even man's reason, to be. No political philosophy will approach perfect reason, but I would suggest that we might pursue the answers to some of the classical questions of political philosophy and at the same time determine what would be the principal relations of a balanced and equitable political community by returning to what was Aristotle's third and highest level of reason. I believe that we can do this by linking the capacity for reason to the location of a citizenry's individuals upon the continua of the objective and, more important, the subjective criteria that I have introduced.

We know, of course, that the intellectual acceptance of reason as a guidepost for human behavior has risen and fallen during different periods. Indeed, one of the purposes of suggesting the outlines of a political philosophy based upon relativistic human psychology is that such a theory should contribute to an understanding of that mysterious but nonetheless very natural human order that can be comprehended by human reason. Again, in one sense at least, what I mean and what I think Aristotle meant by reason is a kind of understanding of, and a oneness with, that natural order, and I would hope that a corresponding acceptance of the use of human reason in the very process of divining that underlying order might be assisted by the present search for a new political philosophy. Two fundamental propositions, then,—the belief in the existence of a natural order and a hope for a renewal of the belief in the human capacity to comprehend that order,—become deeply intertwined.

I would suggest that the questions that surround human perception and the questions that surround the discovery within human society of the places from which that perception grows are necessary inquiries for any systematic study of political philosophy. I would argue that the introduction of a relativistic variable, that is, *the idea that human perception comes from all locations along that horizontal continuum of subjectivity,* only enhances the importance of the second proposition. In the very explication of both order and reason, I suggest that a theory of relativistic human psychology that tells us exactly what the differing human perceptions are and how they color our individual perceptions of reason and political justice should permit us to understand something that we have not understood before.

In Chapter 2, we shall discuss the specifics of what make up the differences in human psychologies that are relevant for differing philosophical perspectives. At this point, however, we should review some of the history of the philosophical quest for both reason and political justice as well as discuss the current arguments in social and political theory in terms that emphasize the role of an emerging relativity. We know that the central questions of philosophy have always been surrounded by perceptions of human nature. I shall attempt to show how different human psychologies and their corresponding views of human nature have wound their way through Western philosophy. In doing so, however, the primary purpose is to show how *different* human psychologies have played very different roles in the evolution of the Western philosophical strain.

Later on, this work will offer a general theory of what the admixture of human logic and human psychologies has brought to the history of Western philosophy. Again, what I will stress is the role of the different human psychological bearings; specifically, we will look at how the role of psychology emerged ever more strongly over time in Western philosophy. It emerged with such strength, perhaps, precisely because different psychologies were increasingly impacting upon the logical intellectual distinctions that traditionally separated the great schools of Western philosophy.

In short, though the human nature question has always been at the core of philosophy, it is clear that at the level of differentiating between orientations and at the level of whether an actual theory of differences within philosophical orientation must include an analysis of psychology, human nature has traditionally been assumed to be quite singular. To be sure, from the time of Plato's gold, silver, and bronze man, there have been references to some notion of the different kinds of people that make up a society. Yet, even these references were rarely accompanied by a corresponding accounting for the actual differences in how philosophical orientation is affected by different human psychologies.

Again, the analysis that I favor here emphasizes two levels: both the role of various psychologies within the dominant strains of Western thought (including the absence of any consciousness of how a relativity of psychology was affecting that thought) and a review of some current philosophical questions within political and social theory and how a theory of psychological relativity should now be a part of those debates. Let me begin with the current discussion, for the status of orientations in political and social theory reflect very nicely both the evolved history of

Western thought and the current kinds of questions that lead toward a relativistic solution.

Richard Bernstein's *The Restructuring of Social and Political Theory* begins with the dominance of the positivistic mode in Western thought and reviews the competing modes as, from their somewhat different perspectives, they made their attack upon positivism. The positivistic mode is based upon what are called the "[t]wo models of legitimate knowledge: the empirical or natural sciences, and the formal disciplines such as logic or mathematics."[4] It is also based upon a thorough rejection of normative theory, making "the constant suggestion that in the final analysis 'values' are only individual emotional responses, subjective and irrational."[5]

Individual and subjective responses are what the positivists are so fearful of, and it is a fear that insists on a detachment from "private psychic states." Though "one can even admit that private psychic states exist," as Ernest Nagel put it, "one can still insist that the only procedure for achieving reliable scientific knowledge is by the study of overt behavior."[6] Nagel emphasizes something that is so typical of the so-called mainstream or positivist adherents, which is that although subjective, psychological states may exist, "the logical canons in assessing the objective evidence for the imputation of psychological states do not . . . differ essentially . . . from the canons employed for analogic purposes by responsible students in other areas of inquiry."[7] Here, again, the position of the positivists is that the subjective states can never be understood objectively, and therefore the distinction between fact and value is permanent and irreconcilable.

A further question, of course, concerns the matter of ideological bias in the choice of political and social theory. The empiricists, quite predictably, have long argued that anything less than a pure empiricism in method includes deep ideological bias. But, interestingly, those who now challenge the analytic position use the same charge of ideological bias against such orthodoxy. Again, it is Bernstein who, in describing the rise of phenomenology, argues that its chief concern is "with the nature of inter-subjectivity and the meaning of interpretation."[8] Bernstein cites Isaiah Berlin's comment on the relation of such intersubjectivity to the reflexiveness of man's self-understanding. "Men's beliefs in the sphere of conduct are part of their conception of themselves and others . . . and this conception in its turn, whether conscious or not, is intrinsic to their picture of the world."[9]

The Phenomenological Response

For a time, the phenomenological response was the dominant answer to the mainstream positivist view. It represented an attempt to specifically include intention and subjectivity within science, and spokesmen like Wilfrid Sellars and Edmund Husserl thus saw phenomenology, in Husserl's terms, as an attempt to find the "interrelationship of the 'objectively true world' and the 'life world.' "[10]

Notice that even at the time of this early phenomenological argument the paradox of scientism and subjectivity was being arranged in a different manner. The mainstream view had insisted upon empiricism or nothing, or on an irreconcilable distinction between the business of normative theory and "real science." The phenomenologists were rejecting the primacy of that science, of course, but whether consciously or not they were also laying the groundwork for an understanding of social and political theory within something that could still, though in a broader sense, be known as scientific. Husserl himself called for a "new beginning, a new type, and indeed a new conception of science . . . by which we understand the general structure of meaning of the *Lebenswelt* and how those meanings are constituted . . ."[11]

There is little to argue with here, except that I would suggest that we would better accomplish this very goal by a finding of the many different forms of *Lebenswelt*. Husserl, to be sure, was concerned with a bracketing of human or mental subjectivity, a matter of self-reflection. What Husserl's theory lacked, however, was a firm sense of the nature of the differentiation or a sense of why the intersubjectivity must necessarily include more than the search for commonalities. Interestingly, Husserl saw psychology as what he called a "decisive field," and he even referred frequently to physiology, arguing that though "behavioristics and neurophysiology remain distinctive sciences [note the change here] the correlative content of behavioristics points to the structure of postulated processes and principles which telescope together with those of neurophysiological theory."[12]

Husserl was critical of early, pseudoscientistic psychology because it lacked "a radical, completely unprejudicial reflection which would then necessarily open up the transcendental-subjective dimension."[13] Yet, even when speaking of this deficiency, he sought no handle on what it was that would define the subjectivity among *different* people.

Unfortunately, Husserl's successor in phenomenology, Alfred Schutz, found himself grappling with much the same kind of difficulty. He too seemed unwilling to discover the nature of subjective differentiation, although in the larger arena of the natural and social sciences Schutz did foresee a reconciliation or bridging of that chasm. Without extending Schutz too far, it may be said that his separating out of the "second-level process" or the arena of the social scientists' interpretation from his own recognition that these interpretations will be very different is a first cousin to an acceptance of the fact that the *Lebenswelt* of ordinary citizens, that is, their subjectivities, will be very different. Yet it is unfortunate that in Schutz's desire to have the intersubjectivities both reconciled and verified he looks only at commonalities and not at distinctions as well. Schutz argues that something is "intersubjective because we live in it as men among men, bound to them through common influence . . ."[14] Yet that position, I would suggest, is simply not a position of full relativity. When Schutz argues that "our experiences of each other are not only coordinated but also reciprocally determined by cross-reference,"[15] there is certainly a recognition of a mutuality of interest. Once again, however, it is directed only toward a discovery of common ground.

Schutz himself is a good example of the limitations that a concern with commonalities presents, because what he is searching for is an elevated set of intellectual paradigms of "structures" that are free of bias and that, as he puts it, "suspend [the] subjective point of view."[16] I find myself taking almost the opposite position, for in fact it may be that the only unbiased structure is one that *includes* and *consciously* includes all the relevant biases. The argument is simple, if ironic, but I believe that it is only through a kind of full recognition of the very origins of the biases that we so often claim to want exorcised from our second-level structures that we will successfully develop the unbiased structure that so many have searched for. As Bernstein notes in his overview, phenomenology "shuns explicit critical evaluation of the different forms of social and political reality."[17] I would add that it also shuns any explicit critical evaluation of the *perceptions* of that reality and that it is for this latter reason that phenomenology has neither presented us with a fully adequate theoretical framework nor bridged the chasm between the naturalist/empiricist theories and the social and political theories that would oppose the more orthodox view.

Critical Theory

Before we return to a review of some more traditional thought as well as to what I believe to be the essence of a theory of relativity, I wish to comment on one more recent attempt to deal with some of the kinds of problems we have been discussing. If nothing else, the critical theory of the Frankfurt school and particularly of Jürgen Habermas, is another intriguing attempt to get at the nature of ideological bias in social and political theory. It has, rather more consciously than phenomenology I think, not only attempted to bridge ideological chasms, but it has reached to span other chasms, such as the scholar/citizen dichotomy, as well. The Frankfurt school, of course, had traditionally decried the depoliticization of academic analysis, and Habermas himself is very much concerned with what he calls "interests." Importantly, he is primarily concerned not with political interests but with "cognitive interests" or "knowledge constitutive interests," that is, those things which describe how scholars and citizens generally think about things.[18] He wants the "cognitive interest" to mediate between the empirical facts of the world on the one hand and subjectivity on the other. He recognizes not only that Marx is out of date in a number of actualized political ways but also that the Marxian method denies that a search for the transcendental and conscious return to a Hegelian notion of the Idea in balance with Marx's materialism is very necessary.

All the foregoing, from my point of view, is movement in the right direction. Clearly, a conscious attention to a vaguely psychological understanding of cognitive interests as well as a partial return to a Hegelian mode, as I shall discuss later, both auger well for a recognition of noncommonalities. But Habermas still falls short, unfortunately, of a full recognition of noncommonalities; in his rush to further a kind of praxis, Habermas reinstitutes a very power-dominated view of political theory, a paradigm that has a lengthy history of being unable to distinguish between different kinds of political demands. In short, Habermas has caught himself up in both his linguistic and his Freudian analyses of how we understand political theory, and as his linguistic direction searches for "general structures" of speech, that is, for commonalities rather than for variances, so too his Freudian design, unlike that of someone like Jung, concerns itself with universals rather than with differentiations.

Interestingly, Habermas, in constructing his critical theory, relies a great deal on Kant, who certainly was a major critical thinker, but whose Categorical Imperative was anything but radical in its direction. I will discuss the psychology of Kant, along with the psychological essence of relativity theory, in Chapter 2, but I will suggest here that the commonality/relativity question is almost inevitably made more complex by what is an apparent contradiction between logic and psychologic in the judgment of theory.

Psychologically, the integration of variables and a diminution in the importance given to differentiation is properly thought of as left wing; that is, the removal of categories is what the left is usually up to. Differentiation, that is, separation of things cognitively or in the real world, is generally conservative. Yet the wrinkle is that relativism, though it ultimately reconciles, must begin with a separation (as Hegel pointed out); therefore, Habermas's "general structures" (or, indeed, Noam Chomsky's "deep structure") or, for that matter, any psychologically based theory that does not *begin* with differentiation will not achieve relativity. There is, in a curious sense, a relativity to the very structure of the argument for relativity, for the mind needs both to differentiate and coalesce, the first step of which is discommodious to the psyche of the left and the second step of which is discommodious to the psyche of the right. I would argue that the reconciliation of ever greater opposites is the work of the psyche of the left, and though we shall talk more of the differentiation of the psyches in the following chapter, let us attempt to recall now what Bernstein admonished us about. The essence of things is neither entirely objective and physical nor entirely subjective and mental. The "dualist" argument—the separation of social and political theory from the model of natural science—was intended to be a liberating vehicle, and it was overwhelmingly left in its ideological orientation. But the separation needs a reconciliation to be complete, and the reconciliation, I believe, comes only through a relativity that, in turn, is born of both understanding and transcending the range at the next level of abstraction.

Isaiah Berlin said that "the first step to the understanding of men is the bringing to consciousness of the model or models that dominate and penetrate their thought and action."[19] That point is not so far from what Habermas said when he suggested that "the business of an ideologically critical examination of the methodology cannot be relegated to the sociology of knowledge."[20] Habermas chastised the phenomenologists for their search for a neutral observer, but, again, I find that the concern for language and the limiting of the psychological view to the nonrelativity of Sigmund Freud will not discover the differentiated range that is imperative for the dialectical reconciliation.

The best attempts at finding a range so far may come from a subfield like ethnomethodology, with writers like William Mayrl, for example, claiming that "the only thing that can be established . . . from the participant's point of view is the participant's point of view."[21] The ethnomethodologists, particularly Harold Garfinkel, make a conscious effort to avoid random subjectivity and mundane psychologism. But, in their place, Garfinkel wants "objective ideal typical constructs" and a kind of detachment of value patterns within the mind of the social scientist.[22]

Once again, I think all this comes up short. The only real clue to what prevents that neutrality will be given by examining the very nature of the subjective bias itself and by an incorporation of that understanding in its fullest range within the full range of subjectivities. Neither the modern phenomenologists nor the critical school of Frankfurt have yet accomplished that—and they have not, I would contend, because they have never developed an understanding of relativity. Again, in Chapter 2, I shall examine the nature of that psychological relativity in greater detail, but for now I wish to return to the history of the search for reason within the context of the history of Western thought.

Is There Reason?

Let us, then, look very briefly at some of the history of reason, that is, to the matter of how well the belief in reason has fared. Let us do this by referring, not only to Aristotle, but also to the still rather recent claims for reason that were made during the period of the Enlightenment. The Enlightenment, as we know, was an optimistic time, for there was a belief in the achievement of a better world through an improved understanding of the natural orders of the universe. The spirit of the Enlightenment borrowed a bit from here and there, but essentially it represented a revitalization of the beliefs that Aristotle held. It affirmed that there was not only an order to the universe but that we here on earth could both perceive that order and participate in the construction of a world that would embody a sense of human justice.

The concept of reason was an optimistic ideal even in Aristotle's hands. But, after blossoming during the Roman period, largely because of the Stoics, it nonetheless fell from grace, or at least from temporal use, ostensibly because of the Christian belief in the fall from grace in the Garden. But the church, and even Augustine, never fully renounced reason, and when the Franciscans and Duns Scotus lost their battle for faith to Aquinas's insistence upon reason, the place of human rationality was on its way toward restoration within Christian orthodoxy. The Reformation, of course, played a substantial role in the irregular acceptance of man's own rationality, but the ascendance of the burghers and the eventual coming of industrialism brought about a greater acceptance of at least the human capacity for logical inquiry.

Nonetheless, the significant history of reason was not etched in the pages of real world history. The Enlightenment was more a product of an intellectual thrust, a drive that was still feeling the momentum of Newton's *Principia* and the work of such figures as Copernicus and Galileo. These early discoverers had hammered out a case for reason or a universal order within the physical world. The greater acceptance of reason in that world lent credence to the idea that not only was the world an ordered place but that man could understand and involve himself with these orders. Clearly, these developments were humanly liberating in at least one sense, since by the end of the eighteenth century Western man's belief in his own ability to know what the world was about was very strong indeed.

But I, like the progenitors of the Enlightenment, am getting a bit ahead of myself, for the debate concerning human reason was already evidencing a significant division by the time of the early seventeenth century. It was one thing to have Copernicus claim that the earth went around the

THE CASE FOR REASON

sun instead of the other way around, and it may have been necessary, if difficult, to listen to Newton talk about gravity and motion and suggest that there were laws that governed such things. The scientific assertions were bold enough, and the collision between the views of Galileo and the church stood as only one example of the grander faith/reason clashes that the attack on orthodoxy caused. But the arguments over physics and mathematics still achieved only a moderate level of intensity; it was the claim for reason within metaphysics, originally stemming from Aquinas in the modern age, that stretched the argument for reason far beyond anything that had gone before. The result of this extension of rationalism to metaphysics was a pretentious leap, and it sparked a reaction that was not unlike, and indeed was apparently influenced by, what Sextus Empiricus in the third century had done to refute the classical Aristotelian claims for reason.

Let us review the fortunes of the rational view within metaphysics for a moment—for, again, the influence of what became known as the Enlightenment, in advocating the promises of reason within metaphysics as it did—still represents a kind of high watermark for the belief that there is an order to the world, not only within things physical, but within the human condition as well. Some credit for the impetus to metaphysical rationality must be given to Descartes, as Descartes was surely the figure who took the orders of physics and mathematics and argued for reasoned causation and purpose within the world at large. But the momentum of Descartes carried on well past his time, and an ever growing belief in man's progress in divining his order typified much of what became known as the Enlightenment view.

We know, of course, that the Enlightenment with all its optimism never achieved full acceptance in the minds of all scholars or citizens. Even the mid-eighteenth-century favor that it enjoyed was soon diminished by the crescendo of the French Revolution. But the Revolution was not the only cause of the subsequent rejection of the Enlightenment; a fundamental epistemological division that had existed within the dialogue of knowledge since the times of the Greeks and that had again become significant in the seventeenth century also played a major role. That division still separates scholars over the very question of how substantially the quality of reason should be a part of the affairs of man, and with the aid of a relativistic perception we may now be able to observe how the nature and balance of that division at the time of the Revolution greatly precipitated the renunciation of the position of reason.

The Skeptical Challenge

As a part of our argument for the continued validity of reason, then, let us examine specifically what it was that its detractors, particularly David Hume and Immanuel Kant, were so unhappy about. As we do this, let us remember that the philosophes were largely of French lineage, the French typically being the most enamored of their own contributions to human progress. Jean Jacques Rousseau, although born in Geneva, was an optimistic Francophile, a humanist who wanted to believe in the goodness of man; of course, the French Voltaire even more clearly represented the embodiment of the strident optimism of the French Enlightenment.

Not unexpectedly, therefore, the intellectual counterpoise to the Enlightenment found its home in movements such as English utilitarianism and German Kantianism, both not only conservative doctrines in a number of ways but also very much a part of the growing intellectual skepticism that represented itself in empiricism, positivism, and similar epistemologies. What were these detractors saying about the Enlightenment? More particularly, what were they saying about an ethic that argued for man's ability to divine his own metaphysics, with reason at its core, and with the rest of the world falling neatly into place around it?

Let us begin with Hume, an Englishman, an early expositor of utilitarianism, and in the early years of his working life a close personal friend of Rousseau. Hume, we must remember, fell heir to the period in which two rapidly changing circumstances were occurring in Western history. The first was the industrialization of the economic systems of the European states, a process that was already underway, particularly in England. In its original vestments, the belief in individual economic achievement, along with the belief in the inevitable progress of mankind as a whole, sounded like something that the Enlightenment would have understood and even championed. But a belief in the progress of economic man was soon to take a different path, a path that repudiated all the earlier notions of "natural" value, as even Adam Smith explained them, and replaced them with a belief in an internally logical valuation calculus: the market.

This shift in economic valuation processes would probably not so handily have won its legitimacy as a response to naturally based valuational processes were it not for the intellectual spadework done by Hume's predecessors, particularly John Locke. It is the tendency, although perhaps more so in the United States where Locke is still revered as the intellectual godfather of the Constitution, to think of Locke as someone who had at least one foot in the rationalist camp. Clearly, there is evidence for this, as life, liberty, and property, even after Thomas Jefferson's happy amendment, still seem to stand for something rather fundamental to the intellectual heritage of the Western democratic states.

But it is necessary to study all of Locke, and as is often the case, method tells us more of what somebody is up to than does substance. Clearly, the Locke who wrote *An Essay Concerning Human Understanding* (1687) was involved in something rather different than an exposition on the substantive Natural Rights of Man. Indeed, Locke was beginning to question how it was that people knew what they thought they knew at a time when empiricism was at least not contrary, and was perhaps even complementary, to the rationalist position. Locke, though not truly a skeptic in the later Kantian sense, was already beginning to suggest that the way we know something had a great deal to do with how definitively we can prove it. The element of reason, therefore, along with its traditionally a priori foundations for knowledge, were already suspect.

Again, it is important to understand that the new empiricism was not readily identified as being antireason, particularly since it was not out of tune with what was happening within the newly developing physical and natural sciences. As Locke himself argued, the very people who were looking through telescopes or watching objects fall to the ground were the same people who were building their arguments for a physical order of the world upon the logical results of just that kind of empiricism.

It was not such a great distortion of these same natural concepts that had led Locke and Richard Hooker before him to their belief in Natural Rights to also require a testing of "reason" with a hard look at the world. Significantly, however, their very request that reason be so tested made the problems that the arguments for reason were beginning to have more readily a function of the increasing division between physics and metaphysics. It was within the domain of metaphysics, where the argument for reason was increasingly dominated by empiricism, that reason was beginning to have a difficult time proving its intellectual metal.

For the English utilitarians, of course, reason within metaphysics did not fare as well as it did within the physical sciences. By the time of David Hume's *A Treatise of Human Nature* (1739), the demands of empiricism had become a significant challenge to the metaphysical rationalism of the burgeoning Enlightenment. To be sure, Hume's empiricism and empiricism generally were not born of unsympathetic motives toward man or man's nature. Indeed, Hume's desire to create a "science of man" was, in its way, generated by a penchant for ideals that were every bit as strong as the philosophes' brand of optimism. The differences between them was that Hume's ideals were based upon a belief in an analytical understanding of individual man rather than upon a kind of ephemeral good feeling about either mankind as a whole or mankind's inevitable progress. Hume's views were, as he clearly intended them to be, of a scientific nature, and Hume's reaction to the Enlightenment was deeply rooted, not in an overt antihumanism, but in a vigorous condemnation of both the innateness of any idea and of the concept of reason within metaphysics. Ideas, according to Hume, could come only from experience, and the human experience was the source of those impressions that entered the human mind. The existence of the realities of the outer world was something that could be proved only by empirical evidence, and what Hume wanted us to believe more than anything else was that the very existence of the "outer" reality, that is, the "impressions" themselves, could never be proved by simple reasoning or by orderly surmise a priori.[23] This is really the heart of Hume, for the challenge of finding where truth or nature or whatever else came from was the intellectual lever that opened the door to the skeptical challenge.

Knowledge Itself

Before leaving Hume, there are two other brief matters that ought to be mentioned in order to better understand the antirational impact of skepticism and utilitarianism. First, Hume, as we would expect, was concerned essentially with behavior rather than with what he frequently referred to as "contemplative niceties." Though he often talked about the human mind and the products of human thought, and though he was certainly concerned with the higher capacities of the mental process, Hume did not believe that purely abstract reasoning could ever affect actions as much as someone like, say, Hegel subsequently did. Hume was concerned with the realities of the world, and he quite firmly believed that realities were separated from the images of the mind rather than being closely linked with them. This, of course, is another important distinction that, even by itself, would help explain not only the substantive ethics but also the larger epistemological preferences of utilitarian thought. Let us remember this rather extreme separation of reality and perception (or the mind-body dichotomy, as it is frequently called), because it is certainly a key element in the psychological perspective of those who were beginning to oppose metaphysical reason so vigorously.

A second distinction between Hume and the philosophes concerned the essence of knowledge itself. Hume not only was suspicious of the power of abstraction in ideas, but he also held to what we might call an "abutting" or "contigual" view of what the relation of one idea is to another. This "contiguity" is a difficult concept, and I will deal with it more fully when I suggest what I believe to be the psychological origins of such a view. For now, we can think of this contiguity as simply an expression of Hume's discomfort with general theories or concepts, or even with the idea of the generality of knowledge itself. Ideas, for Hume, were linked only by tenuous, bordered touching, and they were linked that way because they were themselves only atomized components, inherently separated from each other and not naturally a part of any whole.[24]

This latter point is a particularly important component of the Humean epistemology. From it we get a sense again of the deep antipathy that Hume had for the very generalized and abstract nature of the kind of thinking that the philosophes engaged in so readily. Surely, if pieces of knowledge were compartmentalized, that is, isolated from their confederate bits of knowledge and linked only tangentially to them, then grand theory, particularly metaphysical grand theory, would be very difficult to discover.

Again, Hume's thought clearly represents the kind of epistemological rebellion that was so pointedly directed at the philosophes of the Enlightenment. Enlightenment thought seemed to flow so readily from idea to idea, not as a matter of contiguity or tangential association, but almost as a matter of what was argued to be the inherently familial relationship of the parts of any whole. Whereas Hume would argue that the evidence for what we understand comes from a perception of specific incidents and instances, and whereas he would find it nearly impossible to conceptualize the wholeness of an abstract idea, in contrast, at least the early philosophes would choose to understand the entirety of an idea and then argue that the idea or the generalized concept could stand without being either proved or understood as a collection of specific instances.

From Hume to Kant

We shall not leave Hume completely, but if we now comprehend how it was that Hume began his attack upon reason, we can follow that attack as it was joined even more vigorously on the other side of France. It was there, in Germany, that a man who chose never to leave the small town of his birth refined the arguments of skepticism to the point where they still stand as the quintessence of antirational thought.

Immanuel Kant, more than Hume and indeed more than any other skeptic, severely questioned the claims of both the rational mind and its product of a rational world order. Kant chafed under a number of intellectual and personal irritations, among them the alleged superiority of French over German philosophy. He also deeply sympathized with the pique of the common, or burgher, class as it sniffed the elitism both of the French themselves and of the even more pretentious Francophiles of his own country.

Kant also fought against what he considered to be the deep ideological prejudices of the philosophes, lashing out not only against their rationalism but also against the easy philosophizing of those who proclaimed the perfectibility of man. To say that he was a skeptic is to offer an inadequate description, for what Kant did for or to philosophy, depending upon one's view, was to create what are still the most sophisticated and ingenious arguments for why it is that we do not know and should not pretend to know much about the metaphysical world. Kant felt comfortable only when traditional metaphysics was left to the realm of the purest speculation; and though Kant was anything but uninterested in metaphysics and, in fact, contributed something very revolutionary to its study, he also contributed a series of notions that stand at a high level of refutation of most metaphysical musings, some of which are often misunderstood as being akin to an epistemological subjectivism.

To be specific, Kant, in his deep suspicion of those who professed such cherished knowledge of the great truths, attempted to interdict the mind-body dichotomy, that is, the dichotomy between the "object" of knowledge and the internal or personal "knowing" of what it is that seems to make up reality. Kant argued, if not originally then at least more convincingly than his predecessors, that since all external objects need a perceiver in order to be understood and that since any perceiver had his own perceptual biases (drawn mainly from his own experiences), the perceptions of what it was that someone thought they saw were all substantially colored.

In a sense, of course, it was a philosophy that sounded a bit like subjectivism, as traditional philosophy had always labeled it, since, indeed, his view clearly included the perceiver as the principal factor within the knowledge "chain." Yet, it is clear that what Kant was describing was not a subjectivism that would incorporate Aristotle's full range of attitudinal subjectivities, and it would not so include these subjectivities for at least two fundamental reasons. To understand the first requires that we review what Kant's opinions were of the capability of man to perceive and understand what he was observing. Kant recognized that the philosophes were beginning to represent the new orthodoxy, an orthodoxy that enshrined the perceptions of the perceiver of knowledge. On the other hand, Kant chose to represent the human perceiver as an intruder upon knowledge rather than as a worthy facilitator or final recipient of it. In short, the role of the intercession played by the human perceiver within Kant was designed to be a negation of the validity of perceptions within metaphysics, not as a conduit or even as an intermediate placeholder for a recognition of metaphysical reality. Again, Kant's view of the human intercession into knowledge was nothing but obstructive, for according to Kant the forced intrusion of an always biased observer could only negate what it was that the perceiver might think he was witnessing.[25]

There is, perhaps, still another reason why Kant should really not be called a subjectivist, at least not in the relativist sense, and that is a reason that a sympathetic editor of Kant such as Carl Friedrich very clearly understands. Friedrich tells us, quite correctly, that Kant was staunchly opposed to the "subjective relativity of judgments,"[26] and we know that Kant was even more opposed to this relativity than he was to the notion of any metaphysical judgment standing by itself. Put another way, to concede a clear judgment on the part of any observer would have been hard enough for Kant, but he was—and I believe this to be quite important—even further away from conceding that a *multiplicity* of judgments could coexist and contribute in a *complementary* way to an understanding of basic human truth. Just as Kant, like Hume, could not readily anticipate the conjoining of intellectual concepts and ideas, particularly those that differed from his, so too Kant, now proceeding well beyond Hume, could steadfastly refuse to approve the conjoining of several human perceptions in a way that would assist in a kind of "triangulation" or, again, a complementarity of human perceptions that could lead toward something called reason.

Kant and Knowledge

Kant, of course, can still not be lightly dismissed, even by those who do not share his skepticism. He is justly credited with major intellectual breakthroughs, as, for example, his extensions of the work of Leibniz made the case for the existence of synthetic a priori knowledge that we still hold today. This particular contribution, in a way that parallels Kant's greater skepticism, is a significant advance: before Kant, orthodoxy dictated that only analytic knowledge, that is, knowledge that contained the essence of what it meant within its own statement or proposition, could be held to be a priori knowledge.

On the face of it, this novel acceptance of synthetic a priori knowledge, or Kant's placing of man into such an intimate role vis-à-vis knowledge itself, masquerades as a relaxation of the rules of intellectual evidence. But Kant was far too clever to let it stand at that, since in reality the very semblance of his giving so much served only as the rationale for taking it away. Kant, in his discussion of synthetic knowledge, recouped the losses for skepticism by claiming that, in virtually all instances, synthetic a priori knowledge could be sustained *only* within the disciplines of mathematics and the natural sciences. Mathematics and natural science could clearly be allowed easier rules of evidence than could metaphysics, since the nature of knowledge itself within those arenas was so different. Kant, incidentally, was unable to resist telling us that he was being generous with his new rules and therefore that he did not even wish to put full force behind the standard of synthetic a priori knowledge in the area of natural science. "For pure mathematics," he argued, "rests upon its own evidence while pure natural science, though arising from the pure sources of the intellect, is dependent upon complete verification by experience." Alas, "even with all its certainty," he argued, "it [natural science] can never, when philosophically considered, rival mathematics."[27]

Thus, with synthetic a priori statements or with the acceptance of knowledge generally, the level of metaphysics was where the hardest distinction was made, it being the place where Friedrich finds that Kant, as he observed, "vindicated the autonomy of the mind."[28] Friedrich used the right word—autonomy is what Kant was all about. As Kant separated the mind from the world at large and claimed that the mind was not itself a part of reality, he could more easily argue that the mind was not capable of perceiving reason within the real or metaphysical world. Again, I would argue that Kant should not be called a subjectivist, for his insistence upon an autonomous view of the mind was made only in order to clearly place an impenetrable barrier between mind and world that would, in turn, preclude both a *singular* involvement in perception as well as a *relativistically based* or *complementary* perception.

Friedrich is probably correct also when he chides the neo-Kantians for saying that Kant separated the realm of norms and the realm of being. But I think that Friedrich is wrong when he makes such a major point of claiming that the state of not being able to know reality is so very different from the separating of reality from norms.[29] Not being able to know reality and insisting on the separation of reality from norms may well be different logically, but they are anything but different psychologically. In fact, in the differentiated workings of the human mind, the separation of human perception from reality and the separation of reality from norms represent very similar kinds of thinking about intellectual problems. This very kinship of thinking is crucial to the argument over the acceptance or the nonacceptance of reason as an epistemological principle.

What, then, was the vehicle of knowledge for the skeptics? How did they purport to know things? If there was to be no link between mind and reality, then how could reality be determined at all? Again, the skeptical answer originated in the thinking of Hume; it is Hume that truly gave the essence of experience, that is, the empirical testing of reality, to the intellectual world. Yet, in "Dreams of a Visionary" Kant goes well beyond Hume, condemning even more fiercely the weaknesses of a priori reasoning, particularly in the pretending to know the *causes* of things. This "knowledge" of causation is what Kant would not accept. He believed that the ostensible knowing of "the concepts of causes, of forces and or actions," if "not taken from experience," is "entirely arbitrary" and is therefore "neither proved or disproved."[30] I would argue that once Kant's notion of mind is thoroughly separated from reality and once the a priori has been separated from true understanding, the only conclusion must be that the human mind would never be able to possess an accurate perception of reality. No one would ever be able to tell us what is causing things to occur. The deepened moat of causation is much like so many other of Kant's yawning chasms; it is placed where it is primarily as a means for the obstruction of metaphysical reason.

Kant and Relativism

I wish to discuss now only one more of these obstructions, for the irony within Kant's writings on this matter is so great that I am intrigued as to whether both Kant and Hume, even if only subconsciously, suspected that the very notion of relativism might be the most dangerous threat to their metaphysical obstructions. In his claim for something that is vitally important to his epistemology, Kant admits that he does not know how things "co-exist together as parts of a real whole."[31] He then insists that he cannot know this because even the mental link between the concepts that set forth "possible experience" and what comes through the "realm of the senses" does not permit us to know a priori "whether such *combinations* are possible."[32] Yet combinations are exactly the point, for in negating this very possibility of perceptual combination or complementarity, Kant is preparing to tell his departed confrere, Hume, that he has solved his problem for him, even if "it [the solution] turns out to be contrary to the presumption of its originator."[33] Kant's solution is very simple, and Kant is proud of it for many reasons, but primarily because the solution "preserves for the pure intellectual concepts their *a priori* origin and preserves for the general laws of nature their validity as intellectual laws."[34]

I would argue, of course, that Kant's "solution" preserves intellectual purity by nearly killing the relationship of one concept to another. At the least, it claims that, in Kant's terms, the "use of these concepts is limited to experience because their possibility is grounded solely" in what Kant has already told us is not worth anything, namely the "the relation of mind to experience."[35] This second point, of course, is the final fillip to the work of Hume, for intellectual separation alone was never sufficient to satisfy Kant. Separation of mind and reality had to lead to something, something that was even more estranged, and for Kant it brought a reordering of the intellectual process. It was this reordering—the claim that the mind actually exists *before* reality—that took Kant vaulting past Hume in Copernican fashion. Instead of the mind perceiving experience, it was, Kant claimed, quite the other way around.

Experience and Mind

What better device for the death of reason could have been created than to have placed the mind ahead of reality? How, under these rules, could anyone expect reality within metaphysics to be universally confirmed? With Kant, not only was the link between mind and experience—even multiple and complementary experience—severed, but the very origin of "pure intellectual concepts" could proceed, as Kant suggested, only from the individual mind working alone. This was a clever argument, put together to negate the perception of the existence of a universal order that could be found in reason. Again, such an argument negated the possibility of a relativism discovered through perceptual complementarity as well.

The Kantian argument was and still is the greatest modern statement of skepticism. And, as Kant fully intended, it also struck the greatest blow against the French philosophes and their rationalism. We shall not examine Kant's personal psychology in any depth until the following chapter. It would be appropriate to say here, however, that I think not only that Kant's own patterns of thinking were largely responsible for his skeptical view but also that the intellectual damage that he and his skeptical view have done has been severe. I also think that there is an answer to Kant, and I think that it lies within the very broader explorations of the perceptual and cognitive relativism that Kant himself so clearly feared.

Relativism and the Skeptics

With the skeptics, to review, there was always a justification for why there was no reason in metaphysics, or at least why no claim was valid and why, indeed, those who made the claim were themselves either speculators or dreamers. This would have been an unfortunate position, even if these remarks had landed within a balanced ideological perspective. Human understanding would have been impeded, but all political sides would have been rendered equally. Yet modern skepticism—the skepticism of the post-Revolutionary period and particularly Kantian skepticism—was not ideologically balanced, and that is something that we can understand from two perspectives. We should know it from the resultant drift to the right of post-Kantian thought itself (Schopenhauer and Nietzsche being his most direct heirs), and we should know it from our improved sense of what it is within the human mind that exalts modern skepticism. Neither perspective is ideologically balanced, as the modern positivists would still have us believe.

We will begin to examine different kinds of minds in Chapter 2. We will also examine current trends in social and political theory, and I will suggest why they ultimately lead to a position of relativism. Let me suggest here, however, how I think we can deal with Kantian skepticism in a way that Kant himself seemed to intuit when he said that we must "wait . . . until in the future world, [when] by new experiences, we are informed about new concepts concerning powers in our thinking selves which, as yet, are hidden to us."[36]

As we know, Kant clearly wanted to arrest metaphysical reason within each self; more important, he was not arguing that there was no order in the "outer" reality at all or that only a great randomness existed. What Kant said was that man could not know the universal order, and yet I would argue that at the very time that Kant spoke of both the perception of that order, along with the problems of human perception and knowing generally, he was at the door of relativism and either did not know it or, perhaps, did not want to know it.

Unmistakably, however, Kant was near relativism, for he did have a strong sense of how "judgments are either merely subjective when images are referred to a single consciousness and brought together in it, or judgments are objective if they are brought together in the general consciousness."[37] Now, as I have said, the singular character of what traditional theorists have called Kant's brand of subjectivism was largely obstructive, but it nonetheless demonstrated that Kant was much influenced by Rousseau and that he was very fond of what Rousseau knew by his own term, the "general will." What is important for our understanding is that Kant was a follower of Rousseau, not because of any particular epistemological affinity, but rather because of Rousseau's specific affection or reverence for a kind of "common sense" within philosophy that Kant hoped would replace the pretensions of the Enlightenment elite.

Kant approved particularly of Rousseau's affection for the common man, whom Kant saw standing as the shield against the mediacy and the pretension of knowledge and metaphysical meaning. Kant's aversion to such mediacy is made quite clear in the "Prolegomena," where he argues that "all our judgments are at first mere judgments based on perception; they are valid simply for ourselves, as a subject."[38] Note again the *singularity* of that description of knowing, and note how Kant continues with that singularity in his next sentence, which asserts that "only subsequently do we give them [the judgments] a new reference, namely, to an object, and insist that they shall always be valid for ourselves as well as for everyone else."[39] Kant goes on to tell us that when we want to regard a judgment as "necessarily or generally valid," it will be necessary for us "to regard the judgment as objective, i.e., as expressing not merely the regulation of the perception to a subject but a quality of the object . . . for there would be no reason why the judgments of other persons must necessarily agree with mine, if it were not for the unity of the object to which they all refer, with which they agree; consequently, they must all agree with one another."[40]

As we would expect, all Kant's examples of when people "all agree with one another" are matters of judgments about natural or physical objects; things, as he put it, like "whether the room is warm, the sugar sweet,

[or] the wormwood bitter."[41] But Kant always argued that there could be no such unanimity within metaphysics. In "Dreams of a Visionary," he speaks about just such a lack of unanimity, and he tells us what he would have us do with what cannot be fitted into his classifications: "if certain pretended experiences cannot be classified under any law of sensation that is *unanimously accepted by men:* if therefore, they would only go to prove irregularity in the testimony of the senses . . . then it is advisable simply to ignore them."[42] This is an important negation. It denies all that is not *unanimously* accepted. Further, if there is any doubt where Kant wanted that negation to lead, we need only look at his next sentence, wherein he tells us that "the lack of unanimity and uniformity makes the historic knowledge about them [the experiences] valueless for proving anything, and renders them unfit to serve as a basis for any law of experience within the domain of reason."[43] The argument, in its essence, is incredibly simple, and it is conveniently built, again, around the idea that what cannot be *unanimously* understood must be rejected. This, of course, may well be the standard for judgment in physics and the rest of the sciences. Yet, as we have seen, the realm of metaphysics, as Kant well knew, does not so easily permit such unanimity.

There is one more thing that we should remember about Kant's argument of denial, and that is that in his attack on reason he uses the term "law" quite frequently. His use of the term, I think, is deliberate, and much of what Kant was saying about reason and much of what he said about the mediacy of knowledge had to do with a very specific notion of law that accompanied the Kantian metaphysical view very nicely. The point concerning the law provides a contrast between Kant and the Enlightenment thinkers. When we begin to examine this contrast more closely, I shall want to talk about Montesquieu and his impact on Enlightenment thought, particularly within the study of law and within the larger context of some broader philosophical questions.

Before we proceed to that, however, a kind of almost Kantian logic dictates that I explain why the relativism that I offer as a response to Kant was so clearly divorced from the skepticism that was linked to relativism within the classical periods of intellectual history. It is necessary to do this, I believe, in order that we fully understand that at least some portion of relativism has, in a sense, departed from its earlier affiliation with pure skepticism and has now "come over" to the "other" side, or to a position that approaches reason within the context of the larger arguments about what man *can* know about human reason. Let us look at those arguments now.

Relativism and the Metaethical Divide

There is a great deal of history to the position of philosophical relativism, although more often than not relativism carried a kind of negative connotation along with it. The Sophists were the first relativists, and in opposition to the Platonists, they were regularly accused of nihilism and a number of the other unpleasantries that accompany being on the wrong side of orthodoxy. But modern thought is deeply indebted to the Sophists, and this debt is owed because at least some of skepticism's proponents guarded both the substantive range and the diverse texture of human thought with arguments that opposed their sometimes too well reasoned arguments.

It is easy to forget that negativism was not what the early Sophists were primarily about. They did believe in something, even if what some of them believed was clouded by references to the importance of political power and the human lust for that power that Thrasymachus and his colleagues argued about with Socrates. What we often forget is that there was also a good deal of relativism within early skepticism, with Protagoras for example, believing in "man as the measure of all things" and that a wind is either hot or cold depending upon how it feels to the windblown person. Nonetheless, the intellectual dichotomy between the sophist and the rationalist continued well into the Roman period, with the Stoics from Cicero through Justinian in the sixth century making the argument for reason, while many Epicureans skeptically believed in an almost random nature of ethical principle and law.

Beyond the similarity of the Grecian and Roman schools that opposed both reason and the products of reason, such as natural law, the skeptical side of the rational/skeptical dichotomy was also similar in at least two ways. First, beyond a sometimes overstated pessimism about human nature, much of skeptical relativism was accompanied by a lack of confidence in the potential for harmony or for a natural complementarity of humankind. For the rationalists from Plato to Justinian, on the other hand, there had been a faith among them in the power of humankind to create laws that reflected universal and natural principles in contrast to the skeptical lack of confidence in the human ability to reflect on rational balances within the natural world.

The second and perhaps more obvious quality of this early rational/skeptical division was that the nature of this original dichotomy has never been duplicated. In fact, since the emergence of the Renaissance, and clearly by the time of Kant and Hegel, the entire metaethical arrangement has been fundamentally altered. Indeed, the only way to characterize what is still often referred to as the reason versus skepticism argument today is to place it within a totally different and what I hope is a far more revealing intellectual framework than what the rational/skeptical dichotomy has revealed. Of course, this new framework must now include the differentiated impact of different human psychologies upon the development of latter-day intellectual divisions in Western thought. Also, of course, this new framework will provide an understanding of the current disagreements over epistemology along a range that is predominantly psychological.

The original grand separation in philosophy, or the original metaethical division in Western thought, if you will, was almost purely a *logical* separation. The Grecian and Roman division between rationalist and skeptical thinking had little to do with the difference in the personalities of their adherents, and they were not, therefore, based upon psychological differences. All human psychologies, that is, the entire range of human psychologies, could therefore fall wherever they might along the complete range of the original, logically based rational-skeptical philosophical alternatives.

But the fundamental dichotomy has now changed, and as the original, logically based metaethical division evolved into a psychologically based separation, it is clear that by the time of Descartes, something significant was happening to both sides of the logically based reason versus skepticism dichotomy. Descartes, as we know, was a physicist by training, and his attempts to characterize and define the social world in physical terms sought a higher level of precision than traditional rationalistic arguments typically possessed. Over time, the preciseness of Cartesian-like arguments made the claims for reason increasingly suspect, and by the time of the philosophes, who in a very important sense evolved in a direct line from Descartes, they were vulnerable with respect to the degree of certainty with which they claimed to understand the world.

This charge against the modern rationalists was, in several ways, a more purely psychological attack than had been made against the rationalists during the classical period, but the charge was, without question, given further credence by the actions of the Jacobins and the Reign of Terror that punctuated the Revolution. I would argue that the classical, logically based familial relationship among rationalists had, by the time of the Revolution, been diffused into something that ultimately spread the logically defined rationalists along a different and, again, largely psychological spectrum. Stated another way, what happened is that some of the logical rationalists, believing in a natural order and the human ability to perceive such an order, evidenced greater and greater rigidity and were thus increasingly separable from the rationalists who demanded less precision in their beliefs. The emerging distinction, I suggest, is best understood in psychological terms, and it is a distinction that increasingly obviated the logical consistency within the rational view.

Just as certainly, something very similar happened on the other side of the original, logically based metaethical division. Though early skepticism fully included relativity, I have found nothing that better explains both what happened to that relativity in its later stages and what it meant philosophically than what Walter Hollitscher said about Albert Einstein and the general theory of relativity as it developed within the physical sciences. "Basic relativity," he said, "does not at all conflict with the epistemology according to which man by his relative knowledge continually approaches absolute truth."[44] It is a profound statement, and it evidences the kind of thinking that also signals an awareness of the fundamental fission within what was traditional skeptical thought. The split between what we might call the "randomist" skeptics on the one hand (those who did not and do not believe in much besides a great randomness) and the "relativist" skeptics on the other (those who merely did not believe that things were as ordered as what the rationalists often claimed) was a split of considerable importance. Again, this division has become much more profound during the last two hundred years; and, again, it is best described as one that separates (a) those who believe that skepticism means a kind of randomness or nonexistence of *any* order on the one hand from (b) those who believe that skepticism can mean a relativity within restricted or natural ranges and boundaries within the province of reason on the other. The distinction between the latter position, the view of what I will call "ranged" or "bounded" relativism, and the other position, that of a nihilistic or random relativism, is really a matter of "qualitative" epistemology, a question of how the *texture* of the classical or logically skeptical argument underwent its separation when a portion of that position found itself to be too precise. The separation of that part of skepticism which insists on a clear explanation for all things and thus rejects metaphysical musings from that which can accept the relation of all things but perhaps still believes in something other than complete negation may, again, be best explained by the appearance of the *psychological* variable after the Cartesian revolution.

What I am suggesting has happened, then, is that one portion of the original, classical, and logically rationalist position became overprecise in its claim for the existence of the universal order, and, even in its defense of things like secularist "natural" religion or orthodoxy within the law, the substance of its argument ironically found itself at odds with those who were willing to accept a looseness or indefiniteness of that order. At the same time, the skeptical school was being divided between those who insisted on a pure nihilism and the inability of man to know the essence of metaphysics and those who asked only for a *relativity* of the rational order and who thus opposed that order because of its qualitative pretensions to such a high degree of accuracy.

The original metaethical division, remember again, had been drawn along logical lines, roughly separating those who believed in reason or in an ordered world and those who did not so believe. What happened to that division was that (a) the part of early *rationalism* that could and often was drawn into an epistemological rigidity as opposed to a more gentle or subtle reason and (b) that part of early *skepticism* which prescribed a bounded yet imprecise relativism rather than an insistence on a nihilistic or randomist skepticism found it increasingly impossible to live with their logical partners of the classical period.

All the remaining four notions survived, but for our purposes, if one were to ask if skeptical relativism could and did marry well with a belief in some natural and metaphysical order, no matter how imprecise, I think the answer would be a clear yes. A new alloy was indeed formed. Within the new alloy of relativism and reason, the early position of the "soft" rationalists, if you will, along with the early position of the skeptical relativists, found a home together that ultimately championed a richer, stronger philosophical position than what had existed before. Similarly, the "hard" rationalists and the more "nihilistic" or "randomist" skeptics also crafted something out of the other end of the new psychological continuum. In its way, it has proved to be the powerful alloy that all modern empiricist and positivist thought draws upon today.

Again, I am suggesting that the primary catalyst for both the bifurcation within the two original positions of the grand division and the subsequent merger of part of the two formerly opposing sets of halves was the reaction of differing psychologies upon the modern Cartesian turn in metaphysics. I will discuss the details of those psychologies beyond the need for precision and order in Chapter 2, but I think it is better now to continue by investigating what it is that makes up the contemporary state of the epistemological range.

The Current Relativism

Within contemporary thought, I think that what Arnold Brecht has said about relativism is as good a place as any to note the modern resurrection of relativism. "No confusion," Brecht admonishes, "should be allowed to creep in regarding the following fundamental point. The commonplace saying that relativists deny there is anything of absolute value is entirely incorrect."[45] What Brecht is saying, of course, is much the same thing, within the context of a discussion of ethics and value relativism, that Hollitscher said about Einstein and the theory of relativity within physics. What Brecht labels "Scientific Value Relativism" is not a doctrine that says, in Brecht's own words, that "there is nothing of absolute value; it merely says it cannot be proved *intersubjectively* that there is or is not."[46]

Brecht, at this point, was dealing with another of the great chasms of philosophy, the gap between the "Is" and the "Ought," and his general thesis responded to what is still the commonplace notion that science and the scientific method can never close the Is-Ought gap. But Brecht, in dealing with the Is-Ought issue, offers what he called the "transpositive" or the value relativist view, a view that does at least address, if it does not bridge, the gap between different values and the relative validity of varied and conflicting ideologies.

Interestingly, at an earlier point in Brecht's analysis, Brecht talked about "what the biographical or biological origin of the person's espousal of the purpose was, i.e., what has made him pursue some particular purpose."[47] Later on, Brecht also referred to "what role had been played in the formation of his value judgments, by inheritance, by environment, by childhood experience, and so on, down to immediate motivations."[48] Brecht is not operating quite at a level of a conscious psychological relativism, but he is at least dealing with a possible confluence of the Is and the Ought in ways that reflect what has been responsible for the chasms within and between this traditional divide. In this very important sense, at least, I believe that Brecht is responding to the Kantian brand of nonrelativist skepticism, because, in his own way, he is rather boldly rejecting Kant's notion that if things are not "unanimously accepted by men . . . then it is advisable simply to ignore them." Brecht, in attempting to bridge the Is-Ought chasm within ethical thought, is ready to argue for the possibility of developing what he, again, would call a transpositive valuation.

The Winding Road of Relativism

Owing in great part to the work of figures like Brecht, there has begun to be some acceptance, not only of relativism's possible contribution to the position of reason, but also of the bridging of the gap between what metaphysical reality is and what its observers and its participants believe it to be. It was probably too much to expect that the full tide of relativism would follow upon thinking of this kind, and relativism thus has not made a major contribution to social or political theory. It was probably necessary for this upstart brand of relativism, now free of its original linkage with skepticism, to prove itself somewhere else. It had to do an apprenticeship, if you will, within the substance of one of the social disciplines before it could return to philosophy or even to political and social thought through an understanding of "biographical or biological origins."[49] As it turned out, the discipline best suited for such an apprenticeship was anthropology, because it was here that Ruth Benedict, Margaret Mead, and others could argue for the validity of different human values within a collectivity of different national cultures.

Benedict never went so far as to take on Kant and argue for what the more philosophical implications of her value relativity might mean, but her vigorous arguments for the ethical validity of different cultural values certainly served as a harbinger of the larger metaphysical implications that could follow from such an argument. Surely the adaptation of relativism in anthropology does, at the very least, represent the kind of thinking that defined the threshold of both psychological relativism and the metaphysical acceptance of relativism's linkages within the purview of reason. Psychological relativism, I suggest, and the hammering out of the linkage of relativism with the larger position of reason within metaphysics, now becomes the next step in the adaptive process. Indeed, this step too may have already been anticipated by another anthropologist, Melville Herskovits, who when speaking of cultural values said that these values are ultimately based on "experience, and experience is interpreted by each *individual* in terms of his own enculturation."[50]

Back to Theory

Thus, from an understanding and a respect for relative cultural and even individual values, and with an assist from Arnold Brecht on where these values may originate, metaphysics was perhaps preparing itself to transcend, if not to bridge, the gap in metaphysical reason by using a new understanding of personal or human psychological differences. One element is still missing: some link also had to be forged between the specific or the individual values of different citizens within the polis on the one hand and the values of the polis as a whole on the other.

Of course, there is such a link, and my tentative suggestion would be that it was understood first in the modern period by Montesquieu, who was anything but a political or ethical radical. Montesquieu, in fact, was a deep believer in the political value of aristocracy, and as many Americans know from their earliest political socialization, he was also a believer in the restricting of public power by means of the conscious separation of political institutions. In retrospect, these conservative political preferences only enhance an understanding of Montesquieu's thinking as it relates both to his epistemological belief in empiricism over a priori understanding and to his less than sanguine feelings about the validity of general principles. It is all the more remarkable, in other words, that from the perspective of this seemingly more skeptical than rationalist view, Montesquieu made a significant mark on the study of universal values, particularly as they were reflected in the theories of law. Specifically, Montesquieu's formulations of the law attempted to transcend idiosyncratic detail, and they attempted to do this, curiously, within an almost anthropological context. "I first of all examined men," he told us, and he concluded that "the infinite diversity of their laws . . . were not guided solely by their fantasies. I have established certain principles."[51] Even more important, he told us that he saw that "the histories of all nations are nothing but the consequence of these principles. Every particular law is connected to another or else derives from a more general law."[52] Clearly, then, a linkage of some with all was on Montesquieu's mind, and a theory that advanced the confluence of at least the legal, if not the metaphysical, orders of the world was beginning to develop.

But had it been left with only a nation's legal principles, Montesquieu's entire argument might not have been so remarkable, since Samuel von Pufendorf and later even Kant, as we have mentioned, conceded that there may well be an order within the "outer" human reality somewhere. What these more skeptical thinkers replied was that man would not be able to understand such an order. But what Montesquieu said—and what is so close to the modern value relativism of Brecht and even to the value relative arguments of the anthropologists—was that man and worldly nature are not only very much a part of the same thing but that man is the master as well as the dominant *perceiver* within nature. This latter point concerning perception is the crucial step, for when Montesquieu affirmed Aristotle's view of humankind as both a "part and master of nature,"[53] modern Western thought received a novel introduction to a kind of reflexive or self-defined analysis of man and man's position in the world. Montesquieu's thought, in short, stood for more than a simple integrative epistemology; it signaled a philosophical pathway to the element of consciousness or, better, the intentional involvement of each citizen, not only with himself, but with the very whole of nature of which he is a part. There is no question that this new reflexive notion was a crucial avenue for the argument of relativism, and the fact that it was advanced by such an otherwise formidably skeptical and conservative thinker as Montesquieu makes it all the more significant.

With Montesquieu, an intentionally deep and conscious linkage of perceiver with perceived, that is, of subject with object, stands as an early hint that even within metaphysics there could be a true, that is, relativistically based, subjectivism. It is a subjectivism, I would argue, that is fundamentally different from what has been attributed to Kant, and what is more important, it need not be so obstructive as was Kant's subjectivism. Later, of course, under the extraordinary stewardship of Hegel, we know that a nonobstructive subjectivism became a crucial way station for those who opposed both Kantian skepticism and the requirements of formalism in the logic of metaphysics altogether. Yet, as we now turn to the thinker who was in his turn so substantially influenced by Montesquieu, let us not forget the importance of Montesquieu's forging of the reflexive man and nature link. Without it, Hegel's deep belief in both the progress of man and the rationality of man's being may not have been able to challenge modern skepticism in a way that so many now believe makes up the most extraordinary philosophical statement of the modern period.

Hegel

Georg Wilhelm Friedrich Hegel holds the position that he does in modern philosophy for innumerable reasons, but first among them is his epistemology—his notion of what knowledge consists of and, perhaps more important, of what man's relationship to that knowledge ought to be. The *Phenomenology,* beyond being an extraordinary history of mankind's intellectual growth, is a discussion of what knowledge is all about, and Hegel's preface to that work serves as an immediate response to all who came before him who had attempted to divorce man's perceptions from knowledge itself. Hegel's first chapter is purposefully entitled "Consciousness," and it speaks of the requirement that Hegel insists upon from all who seek to understand metaphysics. Indeed, Jean Hyppolite calls the *Phenomenology* "an itinerary of consciousness, or the cultural adventure of human consciousness in search of a final concord and reconciliation."[54] For Hegel, Hyppolite says that the "Revolution emerges . . . as a prodigious effort of Reason to actualize itself in the world and to discover its reflection in this process without it resulting in an aberration of self-consciousness."[55]

From the beginning, then, Hegel sensed that the potential concord of self with knowledge was obstructed by epistemological formalism. He was suspicious of "the concrete content, which sensuous certainty furnishes, [and thus] makes . . . prima facie appear to be the richest kind of knowledge."[56] But Hegel was also aware of why such knowledge was so seductive, sensing that "it seems to be the truest, the most authentic knowledge, for it has not yet dropped anything from the object, [or] it has the object before itself in its entirety and completeness."[57] Further, and with an obvious psychological sense, he argued that "this bare fact of certainty . . . is really and admittedly the abstractest and the poorest kind of truth."[58]

Thus, an understanding of fundamental intellectual distinctions such as those between empiricism and intuitiveness within knowledge itself, along with an understanding of different individuals' differing relations to knowledge, is really the key to an understanding of Hegel's concern both with the "universal character," as he called it, and with the importance of ideas as constituting the primary catalyst of human history. History is ever evolving for Hegel, and it does not evolve in a sea of randomness either. It moves, rather, according to what Hegel calls "the communication of pure insight." Thus, insight and the epistemology that permits such insight are invaluable to historical evolution and they are invaluable, as Hegel put it, because they are "comparable to a silent extension, or the expansion, say, of a scent in the unresisting atmosphere."[59]

This process of simultaneous learning and awareness, or this *Bildung*, is important to an understanding of Hegel, and the vital element within it is that the entirety of this process is itself conceived within a highly conscious state. Indeed, the whole process of change, or the process of evolution in politics or thought itself, occurs through what Hegel calls the "invisible and unperceived spirit."[60] It is only in this spirit that the *Bildung* "insinuates its way through and through noble parts, and soon has got complete hold over all the vitals and members of the *unconscious* idol."[61]

Hegel and Reason

Clearly, the Hegelian views of both history and human consciousness are much the product of an early Enlightenment influence. Just as clearly, Hegel is well within the traditional rational perspective in his attempts to reconcile the spiritual and the temporal worlds of consciousness. But what Hegel gives us is much more than a facile reconciliation of seeming opposites. Indeed, Hegel's thinking represents in the grandest sense what the very process of enculturation itself can stand for. His formula for enculturation is one of imminent self-consciousness, since a clear enhancement of the ideal of the Enlightenment is to find oneself in an ever more reflective and conscious state. It is in this state that the "base consciousness"—that which is the "element of revolt" only when it perseveres under this aura of consciousness—is permitted to go through its dialectic.[62]

The result of such a level of consciousness is nothing less than the product of enlightenment, that is, an enhancement of reason; as Kuno Fisher states in his analysis of Hegel, "consciousness of things and consciousness of self are related like the objects and the self, like the objective and the subjective [given] the unity and identity of which is, according to the doctrine of identity: reason: hence reason is the theme of the third main stage which may be designated as consciousness of reason."[63] Such an analysis should sound familiar.

Interestingly, one of the most unsympathetic contemporary reviewers of Hegel is Carl Friedrich, who is so fond of Immanuel Kant and whose antipathy for Hegel once led him to call the German idealist "the philosopher of war and the national authoritarian state."[64] Apart from his biases, Friedrich specifically distinguishes Hegel from Kant through Hegel's representation of essence and the role of essence in the universal ideal. Kant, of course, would argue that we knew of no such thing as essence and, indeed, that essence was unknowable. Friedrich, although his view represents a further retreat from his usual intellectual formalism, is free to call Hegel a "super-rationalist" if he likes, and if he further wishes, he can chide Hegel for the position that "all knowledge commences with experience, but . . . does not flow from it."[65] Yet, as we have noted, Hegel's own view still stands as a clear refutation of the position of evolving skeptical/nihilist and dogmatic/rationalist views, and more particularly as a refutation of the views of Friedrich's Kant. We can also find significant evidence of the psychological impact on the schism between the rationally idealist and the skeptical view, and we can observe this most readily within Friedrich's criticism of the Hegelian insistence that man, as Montesquieu suggested, is both the perceiver and the perceived within the world of reality.

Hegel and Human Relativism

In a sense, this criticism of the reflexive view of man and nature returns us to a salient point: this is where Montesquieu led Hegel, and this is also where the nineteenth-century nihilist skeptics so vigorously disagreed with Hegel. We know that Hegel himself was more than aware of the divisions between his thinking and that of Kant, and it is also clear that he found the work of Kant and the other skeptics to be in error principally because their thinking was too discordant, too critical, and most of all too single-minded.

Although there is no need to discuss the politics of Hegel at this point, it is appropriate to refer to the full range of Hegel's epistemology. What Hegel offers not only transcends the inclusion of man within the evolution of knowledge but, importantly as well as originally with Hegel, marks an attempt at an intellectual transcendence into a recognition of the *conscious commonalities* that may potentially exist within a community or a polity. This linkage of personal consciousness with the social overlap of many consciousnesses is perhaps the best evidence of why it is so clearly mistaken to call Hegel the harbinger of the "national authoritarian state." It seems quite clear—in fact, it seems to be quite obvious as a matter of both Hegel's epistemology and his more substantive ethical orientations—that Hegel is clearly including man's own conscious involvement within the evolving *collective* being as well as within each private enlightenment. Put another way, the element of consciousness never concludes with either a triumph of individualism or a triumph of a personal will that might subvert the larger polity. Nor does such consciousness include the idea, as Hegel put it in the *Phenomenology*, that each citizen is confined to a "branch of the whole" but is, instead, a "mode of self-consciousness [that] in its entirety of self [under]lies the essence of all the component spiritual spheres of the concrete, sensible, as well as the supersensible world."[66]

This universalism and reverence for a community among consciousnesses, even if Hegel, like Schutz and Habermas, is still emphasizing commonalities rather than differences, is Hegel at his finest. It clearly represents Hegel's deep commitment to the very antithesis, not only of singular and dogmatic authority, but of a singular metaphysical perception, whether it be logically skeptical or rationalist. I would agree, in fact, that Hegel's position ultimately blossoms into what J. W. Findlay, a more favorable Hegel commentator, calls "an upper world of mutually acknowledging conscious persons," a place where persons who are conscious of their very mutual acknowledgment can strive for relativistic reason.[67]

Findlay selects this way of expressing the Hegelian confluence of consciousness and mutuality, not only because it portrays an awareness as well as a devotion to the concept of reason within Hegel, but also because it clearly reflects the optimism that Hegel obviously felt about what even Friedrich concedes is a highly creative relativism within Hegel's thinking. It was one thing, in other words, to cross the bridge that Montesquieu crossed and include reflective consciousness within the perceptual process. That transcendence may have challenged the skeptics who were so determined to forbid such immanence to reality. Yet there is no question that Hegel spanned other bridges with the inclusion of the very reflexiveness of man within a state of mutual recognition, this being a step that transcended all Western philosophy that had come before it.

There is no better way of describing this extraordinary development than by repeating what Friedrich has already said. Hegel clearly was concocting a form of ethical relativism, a relativism that rather pointedly includes the very consideration of different human natures in the perceptual map, even though Hegel himself did not go quite that far. The key point is that Hegel's rather broad-ranging relativism clearly leaves room, if it does not specifically provide for, the understanding of different personalities and cognitive predispositions within humankind, a position that is not so far from what Brecht later called the "biographical and biological" differences among men. Is there any wonder why Friedrich concludes his introduction to Hegel's writings with a specific and vigorous attack upon Hegel's relativism? Is there any wonder that Friedrich accuses Hegel of nothing less than the undermining of the very epistemological foundations of Western thought, particularly with reference to Hegel's challenge of that tenet of formal Western logic that holds that "all of A is A and all of non-A is not A"? Again, as Friedrich well understands, a denial of this logical and exclusionary axiom—that is, an acceptance of the idea that A and non-A can coexist—is an overture to relativism at the most fundamental level. To put it more directly, Hegel's belief that A and non-A are not only not exclusive but may in fact be complementary is something that only a relativistic metaphysics can consider or condone.[68]

It is strongly fitting that when Friedrich has completed his criticism of Hegel's logic (or antilogic, if you prefer), he chooses what for him is the most damning of associations, likening Hegel to the anthropologist Ruth Benedict, whom we have already cited. He charges, accurately, that Hegel and Benedict both harbor a distinct moral relativism, and he goes on to say that the only difference between them is that Benedict's work lacks a "broader universal framework."[69] There can be little doubt why Friedrich so dislikes Hegel, but at the least we should appreciate Friedrich for the depth of his understanding (still not universal among political theorists) of just how different the work of Kant and Hegel really is.

Hegel and Kant are indeed almost diametrically opposed, with Hegel, even at the simplest level, the optimist and the subtle rationalist, both attributes that make the overdrawn similarities to Kant and his dialectics misleading at best. Further, Hegel, unlike Kant, was ultimately the revolutionary, doing what Hyppolite describes as "sweeping away the indolence of those who confer eternity upon everything as it is."[70] Here again, any tenuous Hegel-Kant linkage based upon a proximity of time, country, or similarity of intellectual concerns becomes largely irrelevant. It is Hegel's singular ability to speak of the intellectual dichotomy, that is, of the antithesis and its inherent legitimacy, or even of the permanent legitimacy of a deeper and revolutionary consciousness, that keeps Hegel so firmly in the epistemologically radical camp. His devotion to a perspective that complements the perspective of one viewer with the perspective of others clearly separates him from Kant as well as from the neo-Kantians like Schopenhauer who, we should remember, held a deep hatred for Hegel.

To be sure, it would be inaccurate to depict Hegel with no sharp edges at all; his intellectual thrust certainly bristled a bit with its rejections of traditional thinking. But works such as the recent offering by David Loye that combine the self-actualization theories of Abraham Maslow, whose hierarchy of needs has little relevance for the study of political ideology, with a pallid version of Hegelian "it all comes together" synthesis, evidence a fundamental misunderstanding of what Hegel was all about.[71] There could be no greater error in the reading of this perhaps greatest of all modern thinkers than to conclude that an easy "middle-as-optimum" position was the burden of Hegel's message.

Hegel's genius lay in the very notion of both the creation and the resolution of the intellectual conflict, and his arguments for the resolution of that conflict not only plead in themselves for the maintenance of differentiation and relativity but, in the midst of their assumptions, also demonstrate Hegel's keen understanding of those conflicts which are generated by the differences within humankind. Again, Hegel's position is not only relativistic; I would argue that it is the quintessence of a perspective that is both caused by, and peculiarly open to, an analysis of a psychologically based relativism. Indeed, a full-blown relativism based upon the differences in human psychology, after having been in a sense preordained by the anthropologists, may at long last be ready to enter the front door of political and social philosophy as well as metaphysics.

Hegel and Psychology

In the next chapter I will try to open that door, but I began this chapter with reason, and before finishing I need mention what I believe to be Hegel's ultimate impact on the path of reason. There is little question that Hegel, at a time when it might have been intellectually more convenient for either a joining of the nonrelativistic skeptics or a defending of the increasingly empirical side of classical rationalism, nonetheless maintained the pliant and subtle texture that one half of the early arguments for reason could have maintained. As we have said, Hegel clearly had a sense of the differentiations within humanity, but the depth of his subtlety in handling the sensing of reason by multiple perspectives is only further evidence that Hegel was anything but an "absolutist" in his metaphysics. The very burden of Hegel's criticisms, which he directed toward the mere understanding of knowledge itself, was such that he denoted partial comprehension as consisting of nothing more than "rigidly opposed, mutually exclusive abstractions." Hegel clearly belittled these abstractions as being the product of an inferior state of mind, and he set them off "as opposed to the theology of 'Reason' in which there should be something of the 'breaking down of barriers.' "[72]

Reason, in other words, was for Hegel a clear inclusion of a transcendence of categories, a perception of the universal orders from many perspectives and it is from these many perspectives that a deeper penetration, not only of knowledge, but also of the state of mind that perceives and retains knowledge could be obtained. Hegel's view of reason, it seems to me, leads to a major epistemological proposition: if a true relativism—a relativism based upon an understanding of *where* these different perspectives come from—is ever to emerge the essence of the full psychological or subjective spectrum will very much need to be the place to look for it. What Hegel might well have asked is: What is the quality or epistemological texture of relativistic reason? I suggest that the epistemological *texture* of the more rebellious and the nonempirical side of classical or logical reason can be understood best in psychological terms. As I have argued, that side of the new metaethical division which maintained both its Hegelian-inspired suppleness and its intellectual breadth was a mixture of some portion of the logical, substantive notion that there was an order to the universe. It merged with the *psychologically* compatible portion of an earlier, logical skepticism that did not, as a matter of method or epistemology, permit that skepticism to become nihilistic, randomistic, or dogmatically singular. What is now a newer or hybrid "reason" not only possesses an altered substance but, I would argue, also possesses an altered *quality*. I would argue that it is now best perceived as the juncture of a belief in a *variety* of *differing* perspectives on that very order. Reason, as Aristotle suspected at his "third level," is largely a product of a real, relativistic subjectivism.

Reason as an Aggregate

Recall, for a moment, the skeptics and their notion of reason. For them, reason was little more than the answer to Kant's 5 plus 7 in mathematics;

at best, it was the tenuously agreed to *commonality* of observation of what occurred in natural science. What typified these requirements for reason? I believe that it was more than a matter of their immanence or their commonality, as so many have observed. I would suggest that it was also their very singularity, because, remember, what Kant really wanted to impose upon Western thought was that there be only one reason in mathematics (which is not certain, incidentally); one reason in natural science (which is even less certain); and most important, though very clumsily, that there be only one reason in metaphysics.

Although it is restrictive, Kant's position on the singularity of reason in metaphysics, when one introduces psychology, is really quite understandable, for we know, again, that Kant had already insisted upon both distance in observation and strict commonality or identity in the perceptions that make up the natural and physical sciences. It is not implausible, therefore, to see that he would ask for a singular identity in metaphysics too, and indeed in doing so he wedged himself into the very level of "mere understanding" that Hegel later so crisply impugned as such an inadequate means of knowledge. The principal difference between Kant and Hegel was that the quality of reason for Hegel, as for any who would properly defend reason today, was that reason was an *aggregate* quality — and therein lies the central point. Within metaphysics, reason is an aggregate, reflecting the conscious, reflective, and I would hope even the mutually conscious complementarity of differing perspectives on the order of the metaphysical universe. Remember that the highest form of knowledge for Hegel *was* reason, reason standing at that place where it has itself not only come through its own stages of growth and revivification (particularly after the French Revolution) but where it has also achieved its own provision for ongoing revivification through its varied perspectives. As Hegel said in his *Logic*, "a speculative content cannot express itself in any one-sided proposition."[73] As Findlay described it, "speculative reason involve[s] the same flexible compromise between varying approaches and points of view that is characteristic of human thought."[74]

What becomes clear is that the very realignment that altered the original, logically based metaethical schools of reason and skepticism did not ultimately impair either side of the argument. Relativism was preserved, not destroyed, as the new ally of nonempirical and nonsingular rationalism and, in fact, relativism, under the tutelage of Hegel, may have been the principal preserver of that portion of the original rational view. I would argue that these preservations were achieved, even in Hegel's time, because the quality of reason in Hegel was allowed to be supple and malleable, an alloy of different substances, even if it was not yet perceived to be an aggregate. Included within that alloy was both the original belief in a human and metaphysical order and a belief that that order and our aggregated perception of it may themselves be relativistic in their very nature.

Of course, the rejection of the Western notion that all of A is A is logically relativistic, but I would suggest that what Hegel sensed was that it was also relativistic in its psychologic as well. Remember, again, that Hegel's chief adversary, Kant, had already acknowledged the importance of relativism, in that Kant's negation of the ability to divine metaphysics was based upon the impossibility of some ultimate complementarity among human perspectives (the unanimity-and-uniformity position). Hegel's intellectual procedure of negation (in the area of logical proof), though seemingly so similar in a logical sense, was never turned into an argument for not knowing. Indeed, it was turned into a negation of only the *singularity* and of the *preciseness* of empirical reason, of nihilistic skepticism, and of A and non-A never being able to exist side by side.

Again, Hegel's relativism was philosophy at its highest calling, for it demanded, among other things, that there be an ultimate reintroduction of the question of human nature (or, better, natures) into philosophy and a restoration of the concept of the very dissimilarities among human perspectives into the center of the stage of normative political theory. It also required, incidentally, that the very quality of reason be perceived as the aggregate of the conjoined perceptions of a polity. Though Hegel's understandings of psychology were inadequate and therefore not specific as to how the conjoined reasons would be richer even than the melding of those that are similar, Hegel clearly included all of humankind as a part of the perception of reason. Any differences among us could serve, therefore, not as the end, but as the beginning of the new aggregate of a theory of human relativism.

NOTES

1. Ernest R. Barker, trans., *The Politics of Aristotle* (Oxford: Clarendon Press, 1950), p. 214.
2. Ibid.
3. Ibid.
4. Richard J. Bernstein, ed., *The Restructuring of Social and Political Theory* (Philadelphia: University of Pennsylvania Press, 1976), p. 5.
5. Ibid., p. 53.
6. Ibid., p. 37.
7. Ibid.
8. Ibid., p. 59.
9. Ibid., p. 61.
10. Edmund Husserl, *The Crises of European Sciences and Transcendental Phenomenology* (Evanston, Ill.: Northwestern University Press, 1970), p. 131.
11. Bernstein, *The Restructuring of Theory*, p. 130.
12. Husserl, *The Crises,* p. 25.
13. Ibid., p. 211.
14. Alfred Schutz, *Collected Works* (The Hague: M. Nijhoff, 1962), vol. 1, p. 10.
15. Ibid., vol. 2, p. 30.
16. Ibid., vol. 1, p. 248.
17. Bernstein, *The Restructuring of Theory*, p. 168.
18. Jürgen Habermas, *Knowledge and Human Interests* (Boston: Beacon Press, 1971) pp. 196–97.
19. Bernstein, *The Restructuring of Theory*, p. 233.
20. Ibid., p. 208.
21. See William W. Mayrl, "Ethnomethodology: Sociology without Society?" in Fred R. Dallmayr and Thomas A. McCarthy, eds., *Understanding and Social Inquiry* (Notre Dame, Ind.: University of Notre Dame Press, 1977), pp. 262–79.
22. See Harold Garfinkel, "What Is Ethnomethodology?" in ibid., pp. 240–61.
23. Robert Fendel Anderson, *Hume's First Principles* (Lincoln: University of Nebraska Press, 1966), pp. 60–61.
24. Ibid., p. 14.
25. Immanuel Kant, "Prolegomena," in Carl J. Friedrich, ed., *The Philosophy of Kant,* Introduction (New York: Modern Library, 1949), p. 77.
26. Carl J. Friedrich, ed., *The Philosophy of Kant* (New York: Modern Library, 1949), p. xxix.
27. Kant, "Prolegomena," p. 93.
28. Friedrich, p. xii.
29. Ibid., p. xxxviii.

30. Immanuel Kant, "Dreams of a Visionary," in Friedrich, *Philosophy of Kant*, p. 19.
31. Kant, "Prolegomena," p. 83.
32. Ibid., p. 85 (Emphasis mine.)
33. Ibid.
34. Ibid.
35. Ibid.
36. Kant, "Dreams of a Visionary," p. 20.
37. Ibid., p. 76.
38. Ibid., p. 71.
39. Ibid.
40. Ibid.
41. Ibid., p. 72.
42. Ibid., p. 21. (Emphasis mine.)
43. Ibid.
44. Hillaire Cuny, *Albert Einstein: The Man and His Theories* (Greenwich, Conn.: Fawcett, 1962), p. 42.
45. Arnold Brecht, *Political Theory* (Princeton, N.J.: Princeton University Press, 1959), p. 125.
46. Ibid. (Emphasis mine.)
47. Ibid., pp. 121–22.
48. Ibid., p. 122.
49. Ibid., p. 121.
50. Melville J. Herskovits, "Cultural Relativism and Cultural Values," in John Ladd, ed, *Ethical Relativism* (Belmont, Calif.: Wadsworth, 1973), p. 61. (Emphasis mine.)
51. Baron de Montesquieu, *The Spirit of the Laws*, in Melvin Richter, ed., *The Political Theory of Montesquieu* (Cambridge: Cambridge University Press, 1977), p. 170.
52. Ibid.
53. Wolfgang Friedmann, *Legal Theory* (London: Stevens and Sons, 1953), p. 9.
54. Jean Hyppolite, *Studies on Marx and Hegel* (New York: Basic Books, 1969), p. 23.
55. Ibid., p. 55.
56. G. W. F. Hegel, *The Phenomenology of Mind*, trans. J. B. Baillie (London: George Allen and Unwin, 1949), p. 149.
57. Ibid.
58. Ibid.
59. Hyppolite, *Studies*, p. 42.
60. Ibid., p. 53.
61. Ibid. (Emphasis mine.)
62. Ibid., p. 51.

63. Carl J. Friedrich, ed., *The Philosophy of Hegel* (New York: Modern Library, 1953), p. xxvi.
64. Ibid., p. xxii.
65. Ibid., pp. xxxv and xxvii.
66. Hyppolite, *Studies,* p. 57.
67. J. N. Findlay, *Hegel: A Re-examination* (New York: Oxford University Press, 1958), p. 97.
68. Friedrich, *Philosophy of Hegel,* p. xlii.
69. Ibid., p. lxiii.
70. Hyppolite, *Studies,* p. 39.
71. David Loye, *The Leadership Passion* (Los Angeles: Jossey-Bass, 1979).
72. Findlay, *Hegel,* p. 29.
73. Ibid., p. 67.
74. Ibid.

CHAPTER TWO

The Psychology of the Theory

Let us restate that what we mean by reason is more than simply some metaphysical quality in the abstract. It is, more directly, a matter of the aggregate perceptions that stem from the working of different kinds of human minds. Reason in the singular is each person's perception of, and identification with, the human order; reason in the aggregate does more than acknowledge the difference in those perceptions. It suggests that in their complementarity they are capable of achieving a higher abstraction in human reasoning.

If it is reason in this aggregate sense that we are looking for and if we know that relativism, when it is other than randomness, can be a compatriot for that reason, we should get ahead with determining what the essence of that relativism is. In terms of the new metaethical alliances, we are turning the axis, divining reason from more than the primary or vertical considerations that make up Aristotle's primary step to a third level perception of the human order. We do this knowing that in modern intellectual history it was only rather recently that psychology was separated from philosophy and that only very recently has psychology matured to the point where it might offer reconciliation.

From a milestone of psychology and politics research that was born of an attempt to explain some of the most brutal human conduct in history, the remarriage of psychology with ideology was begun. The work was *The Authoritarian Personality,* and flawed as it was in its method, it still stands as perhaps the finest single contribution to the modern subdiscipline of political psychology.¹ My own book, *The Anti-Authoritarian Personality*, a modest effort by comparison, did attempt to respond to the largest nonmethodological criticism of the original work, for until then, there had been no systematic attempt to determine whether the authoritarian model could be extended to the political left.²

Much of the confusion of the original work, as well as within the succeeding attempts to both criticize and improve the original model, was the result of an inability to understand that there were not one but two distinct variables operating within the quality of authoritarianism. They were, as Roger Brown at Harvard labeled them, the construct variable, having to with *what* it is that you believe, and the style variable, having to do with *how* it is that you believe in what you do.³ The construct variable, in other words, is a matter that could be related to the traditional left-to-right political continuum; the style variable would better be related to the dogmatism, opinionation, and general rigidity of viewpoint that Milton Rokeach tested for in *The Open and Closed Mind*.⁴ Perhaps the most unfortunate of the methodological errors of *The Authoritarian Personality* was that its chief instrument, the frequently cited F-scale, indiscriminately combined the construct and the style variables and therefore left an obstacle in the path of those seeking a full-range psychological model that paralleled the traditional left-to-right political continuum.

What I first attempted to do with *The Anti-Authoritarian Personality* was to sort out the construct from the style variables and, after placing the style variable aside, to determine if the construct variables of the F-scale—that is, those variables which determine what someone believes—were duplicable, in reverse, at the opposite end of an assimilated psychopolitical spectrum. Roughly speaking, the traits of (a) need for power, (b) need for order, (c) need to repress impulse, and (d) need to repress introspectiveness did coincide, in reverse, with left-wing political views just as the original traits served as the heart of the F-scale's construct variables on the Right. From this perspective we could start, I thought, to better understand the linkage of key personality traits and political ideology as they corresponded all the way across the political spectrum. We might also be able to fully incorporate psychological relativism into value relativism and, thus, into the larger questions of political or metaphysical theory.

The Psychological Variable Reexamined

We begin, then, with an assumption that the range of human values and the perceptual relativism that we find in Hegel or even Brecht stem, at least in part, from the existence of a range of human psychologies. I say that with a substantial reservation about the adequacy of my own completion of the authoritarian model, for the personality traits that were sorted out there as part of the construct or left-to-right variables may be only part of some more generalized characteristic that is becoming increasingly visible within the traditional psychology and politics literature. It is doubtful, in other words, whether concepts such as power and order, both of which are tired expressions within traditional political psychology as well within what is broadly understood as the "behavioral" sciences, will ultimately be of much help to us. Part of my reservation stems from the definitional ambiguities of the terms themselves, because, in a broad sense, actors from throughout the political spectrum can be interpreted as arguing for their own, though usually poorly defined, kinds of order and power. But beyond the ability of these terms to differentiate clearly between Left and Right, the terms also lack both the immediacy and the precision that a robust psychopolitical model deserves. To proceed beyond such understandings, newer concepts will have to offer at least two attributes that we do not presently have in our models, one extending the analysis beyond psychology to physiology and the other improving the quality of the very definitions that we use for the linkage between the psychological and the political variables.

The Physiological Linkage

First, as many have already said, we should prepare ourselves for the theoretical implications of improved psychophysiological understandings. Freud, of course, foresaw such a tie, and the work of researchers like Hans Eysenck and C. D. Darlington is now being supplemented by a great deal of work on everything from brain hemispheres to body chemistry. Early on, Darlington had reported extensively on the relationship between low tolerances for extreme stimuli such as noise and pain and the tendency toward having an introverted personality. The introverted or the self-relating psyche seems to have a lower tolerance for external physiological intrusions and is thus less willing to permit the external world to interfere with internally generated stimuli. Eysenck, in his concern with the well-traveled extroversion-introversion dimension, explains the central physiological variable as one of cortical stimulus or level of arousal.[5] He defines "cortical stimulus equilibriums" as balance keepers that not only identify a tolerance limit for external stimulation but also confirm the existence of a kind of average of each psyche's comfortable level of stimulation.[6] Eysenck's conclusions about a preferred level or midrange of cortical arousal seems well suited indeed to the development of a political theory based upon relative physiopsychological means and variances within humanity as a whole.

The most recent Eysenck findings argue that as much as 65 percent of political ideology is a result of heredity and that such a finding lends credence to the study of statics within psychopolitical relationships.[7] Eysenck is very perceptive in his intellectual history and is aware that the position of the Left was traditionally one that supported the evolutionary view. I would argue that, just as the stretch to a recognition of differences is initially more difficult for the entire relativism argument, it is ultimately a more satisfactory position for the left-of-center view to hold that transgenerational differences exist in the psychology of the population. Eysenck is at the frontier in recognizing that the midbrain, the hindbrain, the limbic system, and reticular formations are strong determinants of relative cognitive processes. That these processes have had a great effect on human thinking contributes greatly to the understanding of something as important as political ideology.

In a real sense, as the "hard" research moves along, the Freudian suppositions about the linkage of psychology and physiology are proving to be true. The relevant range of traits that people like Darlington, Eysenck, and others are dealing with relates well to the valuational ranges that make up the aggregate reason in both metaphysics and political ideology. It is true that when Eysenck argued for a configuration of construct and style traits—that is, where stylistic rigidity becomes greater at both extremes of the psychopolitical continuum—Eysenck took a position that, in view of the findings of *The Authoritarian Personality*, seemed more critical of the Left. But such a view, rather, assists the Left as well as the argument for a full relativity, for to concede that citizens on either side of the classical left-to-right continuum are capable of stylistic rigidities may serve as the critical backbone of a theory of full psychological relativity and thus foster a sounder set of arguments for the political left than what we have had before.

In short, before we come to understand which perceptions and which cognitive processes make up the aggregate reason, that is, before we comprehend the link between different parts of the relative aggregate perception in the population, we will still have to inform ourselves far better about what the inherent differences in the process of knowing and believing are among the different kinds of human minds.

The first process, the analytic, is usually described as a kind of "taking apart," that is, a distinguishing of the different components that make up some mechanism or process. The synthetic ability, in contrast, or that function of the mind that performs the synthetic tasks more easily, spans the bridges of meaning by preferring the whole rather than the parts for its perceptual convenience. The differences in synthetic and analytic thinking are even more clearly explained as data on human brain halves become more available. Some of the differences between different memory patterns, the affect of alcohol and drugs on the brain, and the ability to draw conclusions from partial information are not directly related to ideology, although they are significant in an indirect way for the cognitive process questions that we are examining. But cognitive process differences between the "sequential" versus the "parallel" mind, as Thomas Blakeslee describes them, are very important for the kinds of philosophical preferences we are examining.

Of course, there are a number of ways of looking at these fundamental differences between human minds, yet all of them more or less conclude by talking about the same kinds of things. In intellectual history, still the finest piece on all this was done by Isaiah Berlin when he differentiated between "hedgehogs" and "foxes," the latter knowing many things and the former knowing one thing very well. More recently, in *The Subjective Side of Science,* Ian Mitroff has talked about convergent as opposed to divergent minds, stressing the relative preference of one kind of mind to take apart and the other to put pieces together.[8] Mitroff's explanation is a step forward, partly because he argues that a kind of relativist subjectivity, that is, a clear preference for dealing with intellectual questions in one way or another, is involved within even the epistemologies of knowledge.

Mitroff talks a good deal about Carl Jung, and he quotes Jung in a way that within its own psychological framework, is beautifully reminiscent of the reflexiveness of Montesquieu and Hegel. "The psyche is not only the object, but the subject of our science" is what Jung said in describing categories of mental processes that are fundamental to human understanding. He called them perception and evaluation, and he went on to label the two kinds of perception as "sensation" and "intuition" and the two kinds of evaluation as "feeling" and "thinking."[9] Within the category of perception, Jung defined the holder of the sensation-minded as one who "relies primarily on data received by his senses in order to perceive the objects of the world." He suggested that "the reality of the sensation-type, in other words, is typified by and grounded in sensory processes, objective hard facts and attention to detail." He contrasted this type with the intuitive type, which "perceives objects as they might be and in totality, as a gestalt."[10]

Similarly, within the process of evaluation, the distinction Jung makes is a sorting out of the differences between the systematizing function of thinking and what he describes as the almost disruptive antimethod of the feeling process. "Thinking systematizes," Jung argues, "it builds systems; it analyses; it defines and makes precise distinctions so that men can be clear and rational about what concerns them." On the other hand, Jung says, "feeling often offends, it satirizes all rules, definitions and systems; it pokes deliberate fun at precision."[11]

It is clear that Jung perceived that the dichotomy of perception operated at a higher level of epistemology too, and I think that he would have agreed with Mitroff when Mitroff said that "at least two sets of norms are necessary for the rationality and growth of science, and that the ambivalence and competition between these sets of norms are necessary."[12] As Jung said in his *Analytical Psychology,* "the best we can expect in psychology is that everybody puts his cards on the table and admits 'I handle things in such a way, and this is how I see them.' "[13]

The fact is that reflections of this duality are increasingly coming to light in the latest research on the hemispheres of the human brain. Cognitive research has now progressed beyond crude dichotomies, the rigid verbal/spatial distinction, for example, now being deemed inadequate. What is emerging is a complex patterning, with a great deal of overlapping and compensating between the hemispheres and a sense of understanding that goes directly to the relative styles of cognitive processing that each hemisphere prefers. The dichotomies are still there, in a sense, but things like the difference between logical reasoning and analogical reasoning, with its simultaneity of processes going on, are now much more what we are talking about. In my own thinking, particularly since the writing of *The Anti-Authoritarian Personality*, I have not been satisfied with even a collapsed, single spectrum of psychological linkage, that is, a duality that emphasizes the dominance of what for better or worse we might still call analytic and synthetic minds. It is now time to create a theory that is in tune with the empirical evidence or that specifically relates psychology and physiology to normative political theory. This latter tie is the key linkage; perhaps a concept that could be gleaned both from an examination of various writings on psychology and ideology and which also draws from a kind of reading "through" of so much of the ideology-laden material within political theory would give us a more robust alternative.

A Spatial Definition

Curiously, in searching for this perception, I discovered that I was increasingly thinking about the matter in a spatial rather than in a verbal way. It was only then—in allowing the right, or the spatial, half of my own mind to define the gap between an empirical orientation and the demonstration of the psychological variable, a new definition eventually emerged. My search was attempting to find, in other words, what it was that the analytic, divergent, high-stimulus, sensation/thinking mind did with its information processing that was fundamentally different from what the synthetic, convergent, low-stimulus, intuitive/feeling kind of mind did with its information. If we need to define what difference all of this ultimately makes from an ideological perspective, the tentative conclusion might best be understood as a differentiation between *clearly defined and protective boundaries on the one hand and vaguely defined and less protective boundaries on the other*. Put another way, the difference may be nothing more than the distinction between a preference for precise definitional lines as opposed to soft or, better, porous lines on the definitional map.

With the necessary caveat that in the real population we are unquestionably dealing with a continuum rather than with two dichotomous archetypes, let us look at some examples of what this all means.

Everyone, at least more or less, understands things in contexts. Institutions such as governments and churches or the social, economic, or even ethnic heritages that people treasure are among the more acknowledged "bordering" identifications that all people, but some more than others, tend to carry with them. The overriding distinction between these potential identifications revolves around how firmly we need the external lines to serve as borders, supporting us psychologically and at the same time receiving our loyalty and support in return. Those who have a lesser need of these supports will not be as apt to look for them in the larger society; indeed, they will tend to reject those clear and rigid lines, which they find too imposing on them. Those who need them more will both look for and even seek to create clear and rigid lines, doing all this in order to better understand their world.

Again, I have no doubt that when the physiology of all this is known, such notions will be understood in a framework which is vastly more sophisticated than what we currently possess. But for now, building upon a spatial model of the relative need for sharp or muted definitional lines, a great deal of complexity and a great deal of theoretical richness can be added to our understanding of our own psychological and political perspectives. Think for a moment of a geometric enclosure, a square or whatever, and concentrate, within a variety of contexts, on how it is that you prefer to envision your existence within the enclosure. How do you relate to these external symbols, and how much do you, in turn, depend upon the lines of these symbols in order to define yourself within the larger world? Ask yourself to what extent these lines are helpful to you, and ask yourself also to what extent you seem to need these lines, particularly in comparison with others whose relative dependence you may be able to evaluate. Finally, ask yourself to what extent the outer world's structures are either supportive of you or restrictive to you and judge whether you need these lines in order to understand the particular cognitive situations with which you deal.

Again, if the lines of the society are deeply drawn, its orthodoxies, its religions, its nation-states all seeming too oppressive to you, and if these same lines impinge upon some notion of the self that you would prefer to define internally, your mind is of the character of the psychological left. If you are, rather, attracted to definitional lines and feel the need for them and for the support that you offer, your mind is of the psychological right.

Let us recall that Hans Eysenck has written of the human psyche in terms of cortical equilibriums, suggesting that each personality has its own psychic balance that is important for the degree of external cue reception that each of us requires as we define the world. But the relative attitudes toward the quantity and quality of these external cues may well be the place where psychological relativism affects politics most clearly, for the psychological conservative will more often find that the external lines of the polity are neither as plentiful nor as clearly defined as he or she would like them to be. The psychologically left-of-center personality will find that the lines of the polity are altogether too oppressive. The conservative personality would wish the definitional demarcations to be implanted more clearly in the outer world, and the politics of this individual, insofar as the psychological variable is relevant, will reflect a need for the stimulus of external lines. Conversely, the psychological left personality will rebel against these external lines, as the stimuli will appear to be too immediate and sharply defined, and thus the dictates of the external symbology will impinge upon what Eysenck believes to be a naturally higher generation of internal stimuli.

In short, it seems clear that what political theory has traditionally dealt with as a matter of values is better understood as a part of human cognitive processes. It is also quite clear that the principal Aristotelian questions concerning contribution and the subsequent Aristotelian inquiries into objective and subjective perceptions are well linked to this fundamental continuum within the minds of scholars and humankind generally. The next step in our inquiry will be to differentiate the ideological distinctions along the continuum of human types and also to inquire into what kinds of political contributions will be rewarded most generously by those who possess these processes.

Within the areas of economic or occupational preference and valuation, we already know a fair amount about the latter question. We know, for example, that the analytic or "lines" personality often prefers relatively "technocratic" or disciplined work routines, and we know that this kind of mind values the well-defined work pattern over what we might label as cohesive or socially aggregating employments. What we also have a general sense of is that the clear lines and the soft lines preferences also dispute the relative valuations or the worth of their highly varied contributions. As we look beyond the notion of objective or vertical contribution, we should remind ourselves that we are not (as I believe Aristotle was not) talking solely about economic contribution in any discussion of contribution. When Aristotle asked about those who would be the most ready to listen to "reason," it is clear that his questions were searching for valuational standards that went beyond that of economic benefit. His valuations understood a full range of preferences of both economic and noneconomic contribution and anticipated the concept of reason as an aggregate.

The Logical-Psychological Tangle

If we need, then, to elaborate on a broader notion of human contribution and if we also need to better understand the range of human personality and the corresponding contributions that will serve as the core of psychological relativism, let us begin by looking at the classical left-to-right debate within political ideology. How has the literature of psychology and politics dealt with the distribution question? The record is mixed at best, for there has been a confusion between what are often referred to as the cognitive or logical variable versus the affective or psychological variable within individual political orientations. If these terms are used to argue for a neat division between those viewpoints which a citizen may hold for psychological reasons as opposed to those viewpoints which a citizen may hold for reasons that are more logical, then the division is a false one.

There are no purely cognitive or logical reasons for the holding of any political view. All advocacy involves the psychological variable in some form as, in a sense, all advocacy involves both the subjective input of a particular psychological disposition toward a subject and the intervening variable of where that individual might find himself within the external political structure. Some political issues—for example, the so-called lifestyle issues or civil liberties issues—seem to contain a greater share of psychological grist than do the traditional economic issues. Indeed, they

THE PSYCHOLOGY OF THE THEORY 59

probably do, since the separation of advocates on these issues is more clearly a separation along the kind of psychological continuum that we have been discussing. But, on the other hand, the attempt of a group of citizens or a class of citizens to, say, increase their share of the economic distribution is often incorrectly perceived as being purely logical, that is, it is perceived as not at all involving the psychological disposition underlying one view as distinguished from that of another. This exclusion of the psychological variable is arbitrary, because there is always a subjective range of views concerning the relative acceptance given to different arrangements of distribution, just as there is a psychologically inspired range of views on the relative worth of economic versus noneconomic contribution.

To be sure, few employed citizens would turn back an increase in the remuneration they receive for their employment. It is, however, the differences within a population over how a distribution should be arranged that is the determiner of economically distributional ideology. Again, even within the traditional issue of purely economic distribution, there is an affective or psychological element within each citizen's views on economic valuation. For example, even within the most stratified of economic distributions, we will find that some portion of the citizenry, even that portion which may not be doing very well within that distribution, can nonetheless support the present seemingly unjust arrangement. Those who feel that way, of course, are those who tend to be situated on the conservative end of the psychological continuum; for them, the perception of highly differentiated rewards is well in keeping with their own psychic needs. Remember that the lines personality will more readily accept the existence of the social and economic divisions within the polity. Though that individual will wish to improve his or her own position, the psychological importance of position itself, as well as the distinction among positions, is so fundamental that that individual may even support a distribution that would delimit his or her own reward.

From Eysenck's perspective, the conservative is asking for the external stimulus and support of concrete reward. There is an asking for borders that will assist in framing that sense of position. That "clear lines" personality wants to sense a place within the polity more comfortably by living and having others live within well-delineated strata and although such a person might individually seek a higher standing, he or she would rarely endorse a political ideology that would undermine the place of status itself.

Of course, on the other side of what is very much of a continuum, the personality that prefers less clearly defined lines will not be pleased with the notion of place in a society. That person is less comfortable with those who define him or her in terms of these gradations. As Mitroff would put it, this is a divergent personality, understanding things better as they assimilate in a blurring of lines, and as we know from some of the more traditional arguments of normative politics, these are the very people who tend to be most egalitarian in their views of distribution and reward. These attitudes, again, are part of the crucial link between psychological predispositions and ideology, and, as is often misunderstood, they are not a matter of rationality or logic.

Logical and Psychological: The Aggregate Case

If we now understand why the psychological variable is always a part of the political orientation of an individual, then it is perhaps best to make a clear differentiation between this psychological factor as it exists at the individual level and to distinguish it from the logical and psychological left question as that question exists at the aggregated level. The Natural Left, as we are defining it, is that portion of the psychological or subjective continuum of a polity which is unsympathetic to the precision of the supportive and defining lines of context and meaning. The other left, call it the logical left, has nothing to do with the psychological continuum, and just as there are individuals who are supportive of a current political arrangement because of their psychological conservatism, so too there are those who oppose it and may thus seem to be left of center in their orientation who are not at all radical in the psychological sense.

The logical left comes from no clear place on the psychological continuum. It can be either on the right or on the left of the psychological continuum as it actively demonstrates a preference for left-of-center attitudes and political behavior. Why is it that we have traditionally viewed this logical left as the core of the left? The answer is not difficult: just as there are those who are not situated within the hierarchical pyramid of economic distribution but still support a highly differentiated distribution, so too there are those who oppose the existing order but who would, were their preferences satisfied, simply reverse the substantive groupings within that order yet maintain a structure of a highly differentiated hierarchy.

It is appropriate, I would think, to label that left-of-center grouping that is rebellious in its orientation largely because of its own lowly position in the established order as being only logically left. It may be "rational" or logical in the cognitive sense for a group or an individual to rebel against its fate, and if the pyramid of distribution is steep many of those on the psychological right will be unhappy with it. Further, some group may be so excluded from social and political efficacy that virtually all its members, regardless of their psychological disposition, will rebel against that order. Such a rebellion is not psychologically radical. Such a position has no psychological commitment to a particular, more egalitarian order.

We know, of course, that what has passed for the spirit and ideology of the Left has often been a very undifferentiated unification of the efforts of the psychological and logical left. Those who were subjectively left, and who would thus be psychologically opposed to an order they perceived to be unfair, have frequently been aligned with those "logical" elements, if you will, whose dislike for the contemporary order is not a dislike for a similar structure that would find their grouping in a more favorable position. Again, the reality of left-of-center ideology and of many left-of-center political movements has nearly always confused these two orientations; as a result, the Natural Left, or the psychological left, has never been considered as what is truly the core of left-of-center thought. The core of the left, that is, the natural element of the left, is the only element that would alter the basic protocols of the polity altogether. It is the Natural Left that would serve as the psychological catalyst for the opposition to the precisions and distinctions of any system, and it is the element that has been responsible for the truly radical ideology of progressive movements throughout history.

We shall discuss why it is that the logical segment of most left-wing movements so often accedes to positions of ideological influence and positions of active leadership within traditional radical movements shortly.

For now, let me suggest again that a fundamental alteration has been taking place within orthodox left-to-right ideology. The change is as simple as it is profound; and it is that, however slowly and unevenly it may be occurring, the traditional left-to-right conflict within national polities and within the world polity as a whole has been moving away from logical considerations—that is, away from Aristotle's primary objectives—toward the psychological considerations of Aristotle's second level.

The short of it is that the major divisions within political thought are frequently matters of a *relative* valuation or contribution of different kinds of human personalities, and I would suggest that the theory of the political Left will increasingly be centered around a perception of human psychology rather than anything else. I would suggest as well that the Natural Left, the psychological left, will increasingly be responsible for the creation of its own ethical and even epistemological justifications as well as for the creation of its own unique form of radical political thought.

Identity and Causation—Kant

These considerations, then, are the foundations for the theory. It is human psychology with all its variations infused into politics. It is also a theory that incorporates the inherent differences within human psychologies rather than singularizes them, as traditional political theory has typically done. Before I suggest what I believe the principal equilibriums of such a theory will be, we should consider how the inequities of today reflect the distortions of valuation and contribution that exist within contemporary political theory as well as within much of contemporary politics.

To do this, we must go back to pure philosophy and Kant and Hegel again. If the essence of their vastly different psychological visions is clear, we should now be able to link these psychological differentiations directly with their epistemological differences. There were, in other words, rather clear psychological reasons for Kant's epistemological obstructions, and as we look to Kant's rationale for these obstructions once more, we remember that they were based upon a requirement that a unanimity of perception must exist among all perceivers in order for empirical truth to be certain. It was a standard that we found no difficulty in imposing upon a discipline like physics where Kant said that "I and every other person shall at all times necessarily so associate the same perception under the same circumstances." But, in true Kantian fashion, that obstruction of unanimity began with the individual: "what constitutes our subject matter" being argued as not having been of "the nature of the thing which is inexhaustible but [of] the intellect which passes judgment upon the nature of things."[14]

How, for Kant, was the intellect understood to pass judgment? More accurately, how was it that an Object, or something in the isolated outer world, would become recognized as having an identity? We know that Kant separated the "out there" from the internal, and we know that for him there were only "two stems of knowledge, namely, the sense and the intellect, [both of] which perhaps spring from a common, but to us unknown root."[15] Yet it was not only a search for a common root of human knowledge that was crucial to Kant's means of understanding. What Kant also hoped for was a kind of "bringing together of images in a consciousness," as he once called it.[16] It was a question, really, of a "fit," an identity or a unity of the set of lines within the mind. It was arranged, as much as anything, either in a conceptual configuration or in a geometric design that would achieve its identity through a perfect confluence around all the edges of the "objective" or experiential reality that was being perceived. Again, the hard lines "out there" would sustain the requirement of having to fit over the hard lines inside, and for Kant they would need to fit very tightly, all around the figure.

Kant himself said, "let us try to see whether we can get ahead better with the tasks of metaphysics, if we assume that the objects should conform or be adjusted to our knowledge,"[17] and it was precisely that conformity that he demanded. Also, Kant said that knowledge must go beyond experience and that "neither external experience which is the source of physical science proper, nor internal experience which is the groundwork of empirical psychology, will constitute its foundation."[18] Neither experience nor internalization alone, then, could constitute knowledge, and for Kant, neither could they *together* constitute knowledge unless the fit of one with the other was a matter of perfect confluence. We have discussed the Kantinan requirement for having experiences "unanimously accepted by men,"[19] but Kant's very next sentence is a formidable extension of even that notion, for in it, Kant claims that "the lack of *unanimity* and *uniformity* makes the historic knowledge about [the senses] valueless for proving anything."[20]

Kant speaks very clearly here; it is for him a matter not only of the unanimity but also of the uniformity of perception, as Kant can permit no deviance from the previously prescribed and well-bordered category. This is a testing standard of course, but Kant goes beyond it, insisting that his prescriptions are clearly the only way in which the quality of reason may be fully understood. "Reason," as he says, "must not approach nature like a pupil who lets the teacher recite what he will, but [rather] like a duly appointed judge who compels the witnesses to answer the questions he puts to them."[21] In a sense, of course, Kant's statement is a grand irony, for the very requirement of perfect uniformity is so wonderfully representative of the psychological preferences of the clear lines personality and also so representative of the role of psychology itself within Kant's very formula for intellectual abstractness. The imposition of uniformity, indeed, the belief that "no judgment based on observation can be considered experience without the law [and therefore] must inwardly be referred to something preceding upon which it follows according to a general rule,"[22] along with the Kantian requirement that judgments "beyond the empirical and beyond the perception given" must bring "special concepts"[23] — are the very notions that serve Kant in his denial of the existence of any knowledge without both a unanimity of perception and a "relation of existence thereto according to universal laws."[24]

For Kant, therefore, knowledge does not require simply an identity of intellectual concept with its corresponding reality; it also requires a negation of reason. For reason, the fit of identity must be exact, and it is precisely that fit that he requires with the question of causation as well. Indeed, the improbability of determining causation is his most challenging caveat to knowledge, because it is the element of causation, as Kant defined it, that requires not only an identity or a perfect fit but a particular configuration for the orderly progression of thought as well. In *Pure Reason*, Kant discusses synthetic knowledge, and he describes the "possibility of the synthesis of the predicate 'weight' with the concept of a 'body,' " a synthesis that he requires to be proved by the burden of experience. But note how he argues his point, claiming that "while the one concept is not contained in the other, they yet belong to one another, though only *contingently*."[25] The example is most instructive: it takes the spatial model of one set of lines needing to fit coterminously with another, and it applies it again within the dynamic of building causation by deductive and syllogistic reasoning.

How, then, must that conceptual progression of causation take place? Would Kant have permitted causal arguments to be advanced by porous lines, allowing a superimposition of part of one configuration over another and so on through the steps of reasoning? Most definitely he would not. Kant's rejection of a priori connections demanded that the pure contradiction of mathematics and formal deductive logic links each step of a causative chain in a contigual or bordering manner and only in that way. Clear lines cannot cross other lines, and in logic the next conceptual box or square or whatever must link itself, with perfect contiguity, to the form that preceded it. The new lines must fall exactly on the lines of the former identity, and as the deduction moves along, each square or each configuration must fall with precision onto the form that preceded it.

Kant, in almost a sensing of his own psychological orientation, spoke out against what he called the "new connections" of bad logic, and he railed against the "pretensions" of what he saw as the noncontigual progression of pure reason.[26] When he spoke of the inability of synthetic knowledge to be applied within reason, he depended not only upon the perfect coincidence of identity among different perceivers but also upon the inability of different perceivers to place their causative chains of synthetic argument into proper, formal states of contiguity.

Naturally, as all these requirements can be symbolized by the hard lines of identity and causation, they most clearly also negate the possibility of logical relativism. We began to discuss the arguments for and against logical relativism in Chapter 1; with an understanding of the psychological roots of Kantian formalism, we can now contrast both the identity and the causation questions in Hegel and Kant within the context of their respective psychologies. Such a contrast should also help us to understand how the Kantian refutation of all but the clearest psychological lines would tend to negate the possibility of relativisitic approaches within the aggregate reason of metaphysics.

Hegel—Identity and Cause

Hegel, as we know, was deeply concerned with the issue of human consciousness, and his epistemological rules for the achievement of a state of consciousness depict a considerably more informal or relaxed acceptance of the meldings of meaning and understanding. As Findlay describes it, for Hegel to have a feeling of consciousness about something, he believed that "that thing must to some extent depart from the mutual externality . . . of existence in time and space and from the hard definiteness of sense."[27] Such an understanding, in other words, "must declare itself as a case of some general kind, of which no case is perhaps an adequate embodiment."[28] This manner of dealing with identity is hardly a matter of good "fit." In fact, it is quite intentionally not a matter of fit at all. With Hegel the very "battle of Reason," as he once put it, "consists in this, to overcome the rigidities which the [mere] Understanding has brought in."[29] Hegel decried the alleged intellectual primacy of simple Understanding, and he saw such pretensions as being "rigidly opposed, mutually exclusive abstractions, as opposed to the theology of 'Reason' in which there should be something of the 'breaking down of barriers.' "[30]

Why must these barriers be broken down for Hegel? It is an important question, but his reasons are very clear and they surround the importance of both the identity of what is known as well as the matter of reason itself. Philosophy, Hegel argued, must allow aspects of knowledge to "pass over into another,"[31] arguing, as Findlay puts it, that the "ordinary proffer of information is of no value in resolving the great metaphysical questions."[32] For Hegel, who curiously was the first of the modern thinkers to find value in the work of the Sophists (remember the metaethical fission and fusion), their ancient skepticism, as he stated, "led to the transcendence of the Understanding and its fixed ways and to a consequent imperturbable intellectual peace."[33]

Again, it was the flexibility itself, the texture of the ancient skeptical position, that Hegel recognized as being so important; and thus, with his own discussion of causation and linkage, the same kind of mental predisposition is reflected again. For Hegel, the building of only a deductive science was too restricted, and he argued, as Findlay remarked, that causation should be "loose and intended to be loose."[34] Even in mathematics, where it was acceptable for purely analytic or sequential reasoning to take precedence, Hegel abhorred "deal[ing] with things merely as units, merely as externally ordered and assembled, and not as having any deeper affinities or relations with one another."[35] For Hegel, this formal ordering is a "defective mode of knowledge," and it is one that "rests only on the poverty of its aim and the defectiveness of its material."[36]

What was it that Hegel disliked about these more formal modes of identity and causation? What Hegel would clearly not tolerate was that they were threats to metaphysical reason, and I believe that he perceived these formalisms as realizing themselves only through a dismissal of the possibilities for relativism. In the *Science of Logic,* Hegel mused over the problem of how to deal with the perceptions of different persons, and he talked about the "spiritual" properties that he considered to be universal as contrasted with those that were peculiar to an individual.[37] But the key element—and the one that comes so close to, if it does not actually introduce, a nascent form of psychological relativism—has to do with Hegel's understanding of the need for a perception of how other people are thinking, people against whom one can mirror both the unity and the universality of one's own view of reason.

This, of course, is not quite a full call for psychological relativism, for it does not specifically recognize the aggregational quality of reason itself, nor does it acknowledge that it is the very differences rather than the similarities among the differing perceptions that constitute that reason. Nonetheless, Hegel's thinking is more than a nod in the direction of an aggregational relativism, and when Hegel speaks of the "very transition and the resultant unity of superseded aspects," he advocates the very thing that the aggregate reason demands when it incorporates the complementarity of simultaneous perceptions within the larger population. This kind of synthesis was a major step forward in the understanding of reason, and it was Hegel—in a way that is so different from Kant—who, with reference to our metaethical realignment, stands as the melder of the suppleness and the bounded relativism of ancient skepticism on the one hand with the residual rationalism of those who believed in a soft order within the world and in the ability of humankind to perceive that order on the other. Hegel completes the fusion of the Natural Left in metaphysics much as Kant represents the fusion of the psychological right.

Psychologically, it was that very affinity for imprecision that permitted an imperfect overlap within the causative linkages of synthetic argument. Indeed, it was this sense of imprecision that permitted Hegel to make his unique contribution to an aggregated sense of reason. It is clear that the impact of differing human personalities has been felt within the highest form of epistemological consideration, for, as Findlay paraphrases Hegel in the *Logic,* "speculative reason involves the same flexible compromise between varying approaches and points of view that is characteristic of ordinary thought."[38] In short, at the most fundamental epistemological level—at the level of the choices over what knowledge itself will be and what philosophy will be permitted to hold as truth—relativistic human psychology begins to make its very real impact. After Kant and Hegel, it is apparent how psychological most of the conflict between different views of metaphysics turns out to be.

The New Coalitions

Let us review. I have suggested that new metaethical coalitions were already forming in Western thought at the time of Kant and Hegel. I also suggested that these metaethical coalitions could best be understood as the result of the impact of relativistic psychology upon the classical, logically differentiated metaethical division between rationalism and skepticism and that they had been emerging since the time of Descartes. Clearly, by the nineteenth century, the rationalists had separated themselves between (a) those who chose the more ordered sanctuaries of Cartesian certainty and (b) those who were not comfortable with such levels of precision. On the other side, the skeptics had separated themselves between (a) those who preferred a belief in no wordly order whatsoever and (b) those who chided those who thought they knew it too precisely. By the time of Kant and Hegel, the old logical alliances no longer held together, and the psychologically compatible positions of the two logical sides were clearly attracted to each other. Given what both Kant and Hegel alternatively claimed to be the state of, and the conditions for, knowledge, it was clear that this changing configuration would have a major effect upon Western knowledge from that time forward.

After Kant and Hegel, a restoration of the original, logically based metaethical configuration was no longer possible. The schisms brought on by the Cartesian preciseness had progressed too far as the new metaethical alliances were already beginning to cohere. Psychology, so neutral in the metaethical schools of the Greeks and Romans, was now applying its weight in deadly earnest. It remained for Western thought to witness the continued evolution of the new and still evolving psychological coalitions, and in doing so it had to deal with perhaps two additional questions.

The first asks what it was that would specifically make up the character of the new alliances; the second asks which of the alliances would achieve the position of orthodoxy over the other. Let us begin with Kant, for though there is little question that his writings reveal a commitment to an obstructionism born of a demand for precision and perceptual unanimity, Kant's political ideology was perhaps not quite so conservative as it is sometimes portrayed. To be sure, Kant's views on such issues as criminality and retribution were harsh enough, but Kant at least advocated these notions because of a genuine concern for the peace and order of the larger community. Such views, at a minimum, bespoke a holistic epistemology that differed, again as evidenced by his views on criminality and retribution, from the utilitarian views of someone like Bentham.

Often, however, it is the chronology of movement away from a major thinker's work that is easily dominated by the more dogmatic of his ideological followers, and this is particularly true when the passage of time witnesses a kind of intellectual revisionism that is reinforced by novel interpretations of the original figure. Kant may have made a neutral contribution to Western thought, but the ideologies of those who followed him are both more pristine and more exclusive than Kant's ever was.

The work of Arthur Schopenhauer, in particular, marks an ideological purification of Kant, for Schopenhauer took the philosophical tenets of the separation of an outer world from its perceivers, along with the dominance of the individual perceiver as the organizer of reality, and built his own staunchly antimetaphysical arguments upon them. For example, Schopenhauer's commitment to a Kantian definition of reality, much like Kant's, limited the accepted reality to only those things that were a part of a perceiver's vision and ended speculation about what was going on "out there." A separation of this kind, as we have seen, made up the heart of Kantian antimetaphysics, but what Schopenhauer added was a specific element that he would have replace any belief in a natural order or essence within either the world or human nature. As we know, Schopenhauer's replacement for essence was the "will," and Schopenhauer's own irascible temperament set his notions of a will very close to the specific thirst for dominance that has, of course, so typified the psychopolitical Right. From an epistemological belief in meaninglessness and illogic, the next step to an acceptance of the "human struggle" was comparatively easy. From that dark vision of the struggle came the attack upon reason itself that, ironically, had been made so vulnerable by the overprecise claims for a natural order that came from the psychologically conservative rationalists.

Admirers of Schopenhauer cherish the element of human isolation within his work, an isolation that extends, not only to the subject of meaning, but to the individual citizen's separation from the rest of the polity as well. One admirer saw it as a quest for a world without order, a means "only to discover a way in which value can be achieved without letting it spread into pure non-value of the world."[39] For him, Schopenhauer's "alienation and isolation are made the only possible orientations from which to achieve value."[40] Interestingly, this same admirer cannot do without at least a partial unity within the human consciousness or the human will, for he astutely recognizes that "that principle of individualization" means that "all individuals are, from this point of view, precisely alike."[41]

But if the force of human will and the force of that will's drive to power within a world without order are apparent within Schopenhauer's work, such a will is even more clear within the work of Friedrich Nietzsche, who was an intellectual descendant of both Kant and Schopenhauer. With Nietzsche, the element of power is not simply the creation of a random will; he wants power to be in an even more contentious setting. He notes, for example, that even the tragic poets at the time of the Greeks sought power and dominance—over one another, over their audiences, over their language, and even over themselves. For Nietzsche, the importance of dominance and rank is perhaps made more patent than it ever has been in Western thought, and the achievement of that higher rank, according to Nietzsche, is the result of the struggle against the self as well as the struggle against others. Nietzsche's only solace for a people caught up in this struggle is "suffering, desolation . . . profound self-contempt, with the martyrdom of self-distrust [and] with the misery of the defeated" thrown in.[42]

To be sure, the frequent representation of Nietzsche as the father of fascism is unfair, although it is no more unfair than Friedrich's labelling of Hegel as the precursor of the authoritarian state. There is no question, however, that by the time of Nietzsche, the line of post-Kantian epistemology had descended into something that clearly embedded epistemological nihilism with a deep psychological commitment to both personal struggle and the achievement of interpersonal separation and authority. Even a sympathetic reviewer like Walter Kaufman saw Nietzsche as epistemologically close to modern positivism, Kaufman admitting that Nietzsche is "determined to be empirical," though he argues that his motivation is to preserve the essence of the Enlightenment. Indeed, Kaufman identifies Nietzsche as being close to Hume and the entire skeptical notion, calling him the "last best bridge between positivism and existentialism."[43] Still, Kaufman did not deal with the psychological conservativism of both of these schools, although Nietzsche himself said that the key to such understandings would come from the then embryonic field of human psychology.[44]

From Rationalism to Positivism

For the post-Kantians, therefore, the end of the link between reality and human perception and the vigorous denunciation of human essence meant the beginning of intellectual sanctity for both human solitude and struggle. For the order of nature, whether precise or imprecise, a glaring void of randomness was substituted, and by the time of Nietzsche, the psychologically forged divide between the nihilists and the relativists was soundly established. We shall review the other side of the skeptical tradition, the relativists, but let us turn now to what happened to the other line of descent, the line that came, not from an earlier skepticism through Hume and Kant, but from those who believed so confidently in the orders of nature and in man's ability to divine them. To begin, let us recognize that there was never a question of whether some of the rationalists believed more deeply in order than others. The question was whether some advocates felt more secure in their certainty or whether the most formidable levels of evidence could be coupled with their proofs. Their lineage, as I have suggested, began with Descartes, whose blending of science with metaphysics was the essence of his belief in rationalism. The positivists believed in an order too, but they scrupulously avoided any generalization about it, and they tried to prevent anybody else from generalizing about it as well.

The logical positivists, the positivists' cousins, were obsessed with the most formal tenets of deductive logic, and although their overall epistemological position has largely merged with contemporary empiricism and positivism, the obsession with method is still deeply a part of such things as the standards of verification as they are represented by, say, the early Wittgenstein. For Ludwig Wittgenstein, the meaning of a proposition of truth achieved an identity, not with some larger essence or natural order, but with the unique methodology itself that could verify the truth of that proposition alone. So it was for the true positivists; they too predictably stood as the most virulent of the descendant rationalists who would scorn the metaphysical search.

The positivists, of course, made their demands upon evidence, Auguste Comte arguing, for example, for the strict isolation of the disciplines as well as for the most rigorous standards of proof, which of course some disciplines did not measure up to. His position is a direct refutation of the panscientism of Descartes, and in his concern with the laws that he believed to be at the heart of the universe, he developed his own hierarchy of what he considered to be the proper superstructure of all human knowledge. Mathematics, he thought, was at the core of the sciences, and astronomy, physics, chemistry, biology, and sociology followed in a rather obvious ranking of evidentiary exactitude. Psychology, as we might expect, was pointedly left out of the listing because he did not wish to have major variations within the scientific "sociocracy" that he was envisioning for the world.[45] Thus, the preciseness of rationalism was already beginning to show itself with modern positivism, though Comte himself at least mildly tempered his own ideology with the early ethical tenets of his socialist mentor, Henri de Saint-Simon.

Unfortunately, there was no such ideological tempering for someone like Herbert Spencer, and the Spencerian brand of nineteenth-century positivism created an even sharper edge of evidentiary exclusion than Comte's. For Spencer, as we know, the scientific model was one of Darwinian evolution rather than the quiescent humanism of Saint-Simon, and, curiously, Spencer's dedication to evolution brought what often passed for an optimistic tone to his precise social prescriptions. Spencer's ethics, nonetheless, represented an idealism that was very different from Hegel's, and the two should not be confused. Within the Spencerian aspirations for an evolutionary order there exist the same epistemological biases toward dealing with only the individual parts of science along with a sharp refutation of those who would pretend to know the elements of logical cause.[46]

With Spencer, the substance of his ethics reflected the same evidentiary biases, as his views reflected a robust utilitarian ethic that had already grown into a highly competitive individualism. Spencer did not even bother to argue that there could be no metaphysics, for in a more important twist on the traditional method of metaphysics, he claimed that his own scientific positivism could support a new philosophy born out of the Darwinian legacy. For Spencer, more clearly even than for Comte, the old metaphysics was dead, and the new position, in a political sense, was what passed for a mid-nineteenth-century radicalism based upon liberal individualism.[47]

The New Order

In review, while the Kantians and the neo-Kantian nihilists opposed any notion that was built upon human essence and while they also continued to disdain the "naturalness" of any metaphysical or human order (thus standing as the heirs to the legacy of one half of the "logical" skeptical strain), the empirical rationalists were separating themselves from that original, more subtle tradition. The empirical side of the rationalist position and the nihilist side of the skeptical position continued to divorce themselves from (a) the "soft" rationalists who, such as they were after 1793, found themselves comfortable with, say, the natural idealism of Hegel, as well as from (b) that portion of the skeptical tradition which only wished to argue that one could not tell *exactly* how the world was ordered. Hegel, in his so often misunderstood attempt to keep the rationalistic tradition alive, was the first of the new rationalistic relativists to borrow both from the relativist tradition and from the less dogmatic side of pre-Jacobin rationalism. His escape from the didactic tone of positivism, logical positivism, and all the nineteenth-century scientisms that were already melding into their own alliance meant that the new, psychologically based metaethical school would have some roots to grow upon, even if the maturation period would be a long one.

Thus, the metaethical arrangement at the turn of the nineteenth century was rather well crystallized, with the two alliances filling out and refining their epistemologies and defining their positions vis-à-vis how they felt about the human order and about how they should present and "prove" their new positions. Clearly, the substance and the method of what Schopenhauer and Nietzsche argued for from one side of the original skeptical tradition, along with the substance and method of what Comte and Spencer said about ethics and politics from one side of the rationalist tradition, foretell that the new alliances, or at least the one alliance on the empiricist/nihilist side of the new divide, were well on their way toward coalescence by the middle of the nineteenth century.

What we should ask next is whether the psychological linkages that engendered these new alliances have become even clearer in the latter part of the twentieth century. There is evidence that they have, for what each new position typifies in its most fundamental preferences for epistemology and methodology is becoming increasingly clear, particularly as these novel metaethical positions manifest themselves within particular intellectual disciplines. What has each emerging side increasingly required in its epistemological standards? Is it not principally a matter of relative certainty and precision—and further, in the case of what became the empiricst/nihilist side (witness the Categorical Imperative of Kant)—is it not clear that the merger of the precise rationalists and the "unbounded" skeptics signaled the rise of the conservative multidisciplinary ideologies of the latter nineteenth and the twentieth century?

Again, let us be specific about the realignment. It was not caused by the mere existence of knowledge or data alone, those data working their way to the intellectual frontier of each discipline. The new knowledge, of course, was the stuff of the change, but the catalyst for the change was the solitary burden of very different minds that worked consciously out of logically based schools of thought while they subconsciously responded to their psychological preferences. We raised two questions earlier. The first concerned the realignment itself, but the second—and the one with which the subsequent chapters will concern themselves—is really the more difficult of the two. It is difficult because, on its surface, it appears to ask nothing more than which of the two coalitions may have been put together more easily. Yet, within the province of ethical thought, and particularly within the working out of the impact of the theories of different social science disciplines, the issue of primacy is really rather complex. The impact of the realignment was felt quite widely in all those disciplines, and although the impact upon politics and political theory is the final step in this review, a look at the social science disciplines in order to see who "won" the struggle for dominance ought to be helpful.

The Left Position

If we are to inquire into who has gained the upper hand between the new realignments, it will first be necessary to complete the history of the development of the other side, the left side, and review what it was that happened within the realignment that was taking place there. The analysis concerns what I have called the "bounded" skeptics or relativists along with those rationalists who did not fall into the depths of positivism. We have already discussed Hegel and Brecht as well as the movement of relativism into the discipline of anthropology. From those beginnings, we should now examine the confluence of that "left" coalition into that position of relativism which existed within an aggregated reason.

If we can reincorporate the depiction of Hegel as a post-Revolutionary rationalist and agree that his relativism was of the kind that accepted the existence of the unknown along with the known—and if, at the same time, we can accept that the burden of Hegel's antithesis was at first an opposition to prevailing orthodoxy—then we can discover what it was within logical relativism that served as one of the bases of the left side of the new metaethical divide. Again, we have traced logical relativism into the ethical relativism of the anthropologists, and we should include a mention of someone like Peter Berger and his historical relativism at the same time that we reincorporate the attempt at the bridging of the Is-Ought gap with the "transpositivism" of Arnold Brecht.

Yet, all in all, I feel most comfortable with what is still the core of Hegelian relativism, that being the Hegelian view of both reality and our perceptions of that reality. This is the core of what makes up the theoretical base for a psychological relativism, a relativism that contrasts with the more empirically dominated coalition that we have already examined. It begins with the consideration of the elements of knowledge themselves, and it explores how these elements are identified and how they are related to the holder of each of them. It also considers how they are all sewn together to compose the rudiments of knowledge itself.

For Hegel, as we have said, the "fit" of all this never needed to be exact, and he felt that way for not one but two principal reasons. The first was that there was range and relativity on the border of each element of knowledge; the other was that new perceptions would always be allowed to flow together with the old to alter and improve the understandings that might currently be in vogue. Perhaps there were good reasons for why that nonfitting and psychologically relativist position had to serve a belated apprenticeship within anthropology before it could achieve intellectual acceptance. But it could be argued just as easily that it garnered its seasoning because it could not, as a practical matter, serve in the real world of nineteenth-century industrial nationalism in a very helpful way. Regardless of why it was that it seemed to do less well at the inception of the realignment, the Hegelian view clearly was lying fallow before its tentative relativism could flower into full ethical relativity. It may be fair to say, in fact, that the left side of the epistemological divide achieved an indigenous viability only through the analogous confluence of relativism with rationalism within physics. Even there, it was achieved only because of the slow acceptance among physicists of the fact, as Hollistcher put it with Einstein, that relativity does not deny ordered existence any more than imprecision necessarily implies unknowability.

From Logical to Empirical Relativity

What still needs to be mentioned before we review fission-fusion in the social disciplines themselves is the essence of relativity within physics, something that is nothing less than an acceptance of the ambivalence of the most "scientific" of definitions. Remember that it was Einstein's breakthrough in the description of matter itself that was the catalyst for relativity. The very notion of activity, that is, the notion of the changing nature of the subatomic world, permitted the relativistic milestone of quantum theory (originally conceived by Max Planck) to exist within the study of light. But the breakthrough in the description of the particle/wave argument was a matter of a *quality* of understanding, a quality that grew from an understanding of the very impreciseness and dynamic nature of seemingly innate matter. The reasoning was the product of an ability to blend a variety of imprecise definitions and to declare, eventually, that space and time were not separate and exclusive entities but were in fact deeply intertwined. What an incredible amalgam these seemingly convoluted and flexible Einsteinian perceptions were! We still stand in awe of them, even with what for the most of us is such a meager understanding of the physics of which they are made.

But if we have been bold in suggesting a model of political relativism, then we should be no less bold in suggesting that the Einsteinian revelation that led to the touchstone of relativity within physics is precisely the kind of breakthrough that Hegel at least held open within his own form of relativism. Remember that Hegel, with his insistence upon the possibility of the logical coexistence of both A and non-A, also ratified the understandings of Montesquieu, who had argued for the inclusion of the perceiver within the reality of the perceived. Hegel was on the threshold of perceiving what the merger of the seemingly distinct perceivers could do, in the aggregate, to divine the relativist and aggregate reason. After a lengthy slumber, perhaps this Hegelian logical relativism might now be joined by Einstein's empirical relativism to lay the groundwork for a fullblown theory of metaphysical relativism.

Metaphysical Relativism

We began this chapter with a discussion of different kinds of minds, and perhaps it is now clear that the very process that combines relativism and rationalism, whether within metaphysics or physics, is decidedly the province of one kind of human mind. Was Einstein's brilliance a matter of pure intellect, a mere capacity that permitted him to see what others could not? Not at all. Einstein's perception, like Hegel's, was a matter of psychology. It was a case, again, of a different kind of mind, a mind that permitted a transcendence over the unities of identity and over the perfect congruities of causation that traditional physics, in almost Kantian fashion, had always imposed. Einstein, in one grand leap, transcended the very burden of finiteness, and he did so, not only in the study of matter, but throughout the building of the theory of relativity and through the marvelously original understandings of the overlapping relationships between time and space that he understood so well. It was the nonfinite, imprecise quality of things that he understood, and we can only ask if this same quality might not be duplicated within a philosophy of the political Left. Of course, part of why it has taken so long has to do with both the demands and the facile economic promises of what passes for radical political philosophy. But there is more to it than that, for indeed, long-term intellectual biases against relativism are why the step from Hegel's logical relativism to a philosophy of the Natural Left has taken so long.

The intellectual positivism and the artistic romanticism of the nineteenth century may have had something to do with it. The lack of understanding of the human brain and the corresponding belief in the peripheral if not redundant role of the right hemisphere may also have been a factor. History's blush of nationalism and optimistic industrialism were significant as well; yet, on balance, perhaps the most important factor had to do with the structure of the argument itself, for once the nineteenth-century empiricists had established themselves beneath the wing of the conservative metaethical coalition, the task of the left coalition, which would have fostered the Natural Left, became one of arguing for relativism itself, along with the position that it favored. The Natural Left argument, in short, was *inherently* a more difficult argument, because it was a two-stage rather than a one-stage claim. There is a beautiful little quotation in the Mitroff book by Thomas Cowan in which Cowan says that "there are two knds of people in the world, those who think that there are two kinds of people in the world and those who don't." and this simple notion may be the key to the tardiness of the relativist ascendancy. The relativist kind of mind, which as the metaethical axis rotated from vertical to horizontal was represented solely on the left side among the new coalitions, carried the double obligation. It always had to argue for relativism itself as well as for its own position.

Of course, when one thinks of it, the arrival of relativism within physics, well after we were confident that we knew a great deal of what passed for ultimate knowledge under the Newtonian model, was really rather late in coming too. We have frequently been at the place where we thought we knew a good deal about metaphysics and politics, but the very epistemological singularity of what we knew was more and more clearly the product of the kind of mind that *can* know only that singularity. Is it any wonder that the attempts to speak of such things as the Is and the Ought in a way that acknowledges the multiplicity of the Oughts has never occurred in a fully relativistic way? Why did even Brecht and the others fall short of full relativism? Again, it was psychology that was missing, for even with his understanding of "biographical or biological origins," he did not have a vision of the range of human personality or of the kinds of variables that make up that range.

Perhaps now, with our awakening to the very physiology and psychology of humanity that the positivists and the nihilists have empirically championed and philosophically feared, we will be able to include both the essential equilibriums of collective human existence and the considerations of the range of human contribution to that existence within our considerations. Psychological relativism will not permit but will insist upon a relativistic metaphysical view. As the relativism of anthropology and history brought new visions to their disciplines, it is now clear that the relativism of psychology is capable of assisting that level of human self-consciousness which Hegel insisted upon in metaphysics and politics.

If we have understood Hegel well, and if we understand the psychological relativism that exists within the human population, we should be able to unfold the greater parameters of what it was that Aristotle was saying when he talked about the ability to reason. Reason is there, but it can be understood only in the aggregate, and it will not be enough to simply turn the axis from the vertical to the horizontal in order to understand it. The conscious recognition of the horizontal or subjective view of reasonable contribution, allocation, or whatever will depend not only upon our understanding of what different personalities think about these fundamental equities but also upon how these persons think about the very question of contributive equity. The subjective is of no value without a metaphysical foundation, and metaphysical foundation cannot be understood without a knowledge of the relative functions of different kinds of minds. Only from these triangulated vantage points can we derive true reason as an aggregate, just as Aristotle hinted in his third level. If this very explanation of why the coalition of the new rationalist/relativist was late in coming is reasonable, we can then examine how the new metaethical coalitions, in turn, fostered their biases within the social sciences generally and political philosophy in particular.

NOTES

1. T. W. Adorno et al., *The Authoritarian Personality* (New York: Harper and Row, 1950).

2. William P. Kreml, *The Anti-Authoritarian Personality* (London: Pergamon Press, 1977).
3. Roger Brown, *Social Psychology* (New York: The Free Press, 1965), p. 489.
4. Milton Rokeach, *The Open and Closed Mind* (New York: Basic Books, 1968).
5. Hans Eysenck, *The Biological Basis of Personality* (Springfield, Ill.: Charles C. Thomas, 1967).
6. C. D. Darlington, "Psychology, Genetics and the Process of History," *British Journal of Psychology* 54 (1963):293–98.
7. Hans Eysenck and L. J. Eaves, "Genetics and the Development of Social Attitudes," *Nature* 249 (May 17, 1974):288–89.
8. Ian Mitroff, *The Subjective Side of Science* (Amsterdam: Elsevier, 1974), pp. 139–140.
9. C. G. Jung, *Analytical Psychology, Its Theory and Practice* (New York: Pantheon Books, 1968), p. 142, as quoted in Mitroff, ibid., p. 170.
10. Ibid., p. 168
11. Ibid., p. 169.
12. Mitroff, *Subjective Side*, p. 169.
13. Jung, *Analytical Psychology*, p. 142.
14. Immanuel Kant, "Prolegomena," in Carl J. Friedrich, ed., *The Philosophy of Kant* (New York: Modern Library, 1949), p. 73.
15. Immanuel Kant, "Critique of Pure Reason," in Friedrich, ibid., p. 37.
16. Ibid., p. 39.
17. Ibid.
18. Carl J. Friedrich, Introduction, *The Philosophy of Kant* (New York: Modern Library, 1949).
19. Kant, "Prolegomena," in Friedrich, ibid., p. 50.
20. Immanuel Kant, "Dreams of a Visionary," in Friedrich, ibid., p. 21. (Emphasis mine).
21. Friedrich, Introduction, *Philosophy of Kant*, p. xxvii.
22. Kant, "Prolegomena," p. 70.
23. Ibid., pp. 81–82.
24. Kant, "Critique of Pure Reason," p. 31.
25. Ibid., p. 32. (Emphasis mine.)
26. Kant, "Prolegomena," p. 63.
27. J. N. Findlay, *Hegel: A Re-examination* (New York: Oxford University Press, 1958), p. 41.
28. Ibid.
29. Quoted in Findlay, *Hegel*, p. 27.
30. Ibid., p. 29.
31. Ibid., p. 62.
32. J. N. Findlay, *Hegel*, p. 64.
33. Ibid.
34. Ibid., p. 23.
35. Ibid., p. 59.

36. Quoted in Findlay, *Hegel*, p. 59.
37. Ibid., pp. 45–46.
38. Ibid., p. 67.
39. Morse Peckham, *Beyond the Tragic Vision* (New York: George Braziller, 1962), p. 173.
40. Ibid.
41. Ibid., p. 174.
42. Paul Edwards, ed., *The Encyclopedia of Philosophy* (New York: Macmillan and The Free Press, 1967), vol. V, p. 512.
43. Friedrich Nietzsche, in Walter Kaufman and R. G. Hollingdale, eds., *The Will to Power* (New York: Random House, 1967), p. 910.
44. See Friedrich Nietzsche, *Human, All Too Human* (London: T. N. Foulis, 1910), pp. 13–14 and pp. 53–56.
45. Auguste Comte, "*Cours de Philosophie Positif*" in Stanislav Andreski, ed., *The Essential Comte* (London: Croom Helm, 1974), pp. 32–33.
46. J. D. Y. Peel, *Herbert Spencer* (New York: Basic Books, 1971), pp. 131–65.
47. See David Wiltshire, *The Social and Political Thought of Herbert Spencer* (Oxford: Oxford University Press, 1978), pp. 24–46.

CHAPTER THREE

The Social Sciences

The Law

The movement away from traditional rationalism in the law of the late eighteenth century represents perhaps the best example of how a desire for certainty within a discipline distorted psychological balance and hastened the victory of the emerging skeptical/empirical coalition. The peculiar twists of utilitarianism have so clearly manifested themselves within Western law, and particularly within the English version of that law, that our review should include the stages that led both to the dominance of process within that law and to the dominance of legal positivism during the nineteenth century generally.

We begin with the rationalists and their opposition to the sophistic view that, once again, was a division in approach that is still reflected well into the eighteenth century. The attacks on rationality that came from Hugo Grotius's secularism or from Reformation thought did not have the psychological impact that came from the work of two immediate Lockean predecessors, Richard Hooker and Samuel von Pufendorf. Reformation thought had its epistemological by-products, and even though they were not so apparent within the writings of the early reformers, the epistemological shift became more obvious in the works of Richard Hooker, the nearly Catholic Anglican who turned the principles of natural law toward the notion of natural right. Whereas Grotius had maintained the commonalities within the natural law—or, as one author put it, where he had seen to the triumph of Renaissance over Reformation in maintaining the primacy of the law—Hooker, though still maintaining *Lex* over *Ius,* nonetheless made the *Ecclesiastical Polity* into a catalyst for a more individualistic notion of natural law.[1] To be sure, Hooker was still firmly in the Thomist tradition in his own formulation of natural right, certainly more so than the Puritans. But Hooker, like so many who are caught between competing currents during a period of intellectual transition, was at one time trying to solidify Anglicanism against the Catholics and, at the same time, trying to forestall the individualistic "radicalism" of the Puritans. His writings on law reflected those tensions, and although his own intellectual accession to a concept of natural right was anything but a full acceptance of either embryonic individualism or its later arriving epistemological cousin, empiricism, it still stands as a benchmark of fundamental withdrawal from the more psychologically neutral rationalism of earlier, Catholic thought.

Samuel von Pufendorf was probably even more important to the development of both Lockean thinking in general and of the Lockean perception of natural right in particular. It is through Pufendorf's influence that an epistemological linkage of the law with an almost mathematical and more purely contractual jurisprudence is firmly joined. Pufendorf's early training in mathematics lends a kind of early-day Comtian thread to his legal theories as Pufendorf attempted to find a rational calculus both for the law and for politics. Although he believed strongly in the natural law, his attempt to regularize the natural law's method and at the same time balance the secular interpretations of Grotius with the dominant statism of Hobbes clearly led Pufendorf into the more contractual and atomistic assumptions that typify his work. Without question, Locke's penchant for economic individualism and his concurrent fear of the influence of what for those days passed as a democratic legislature were in large part due to the intellectual influence of his German predecessor.[2]

Thus, by the time of Locke, the Scholastic and even humanistic visions of the natural law were both viewed among modern rationalists as being both religiously and scientifically unsound.[3] Bolstered by the richness of Coke's early-seventeenth-century strengthening of common law, he was able to bring the theory of natural right into a position of status for itself, well outside traditional naturalist principles. *Ius* was now more important than *Lex,* and Locke, buttressed by the notions of Pufendorf concerning the acquisitiveness of man, was ready to argue for both a full theory of private property and a full set of legal protections for the fruits of one's labor.

For our purposes, the crucial milestone within Locke is not that he adopted an ethic that surrounded individualism and private property in a protective cocoon but that he adopted the empirical and epistemologically scientific notions of his forerunner, Pufendorf. The impact of this latter acceptance was important because it was also instrumental in the thinking of people like Blackstone in England, Voltaire on the Continent, and others who continued the rotation of the jurisprudential axis around the natural law. By the end of the seventeenth century, an increasingly individualistic, scientific, and empirically directed calculus of legal conception was well on its way to acceptance. The potent calculus of utilitarianism may have reached its greatest formalization only through the skeptically derived thought of Hume and Bentham, but by the time of Locke it was clear that the deductive logic of Descartes and the mathematics of Pufendorf were already replacing the rationalist tradition within the law with a more analytic framework.

Nonetheless, despite the epistemological wanderings, Locke still attempted to hold on to some traditional rationalistic principles, perhaps because they were useful to him as he responded to the emerging threat to private property that he perceived as coming from the modern state. His subordination of natural law to a more individualistic notion of natural right than Hooker had proposed revealed the first partial rotation on the axis from a logically rationalistic, neutral psychological position to a more analytical epistemological view.

Après Locke le Deluge

What happened after Locke was probably inevitable, pushed along as it was by the reality of the industrializing world. The substance and the method of Locke clearly became estranged within the work of Locke's immediate successors, though the primary successors to Locke's brand of rationalism often cloaked their betrayals of a psychologically neutral natural law within what appeared to be a strident defense of the old orthodoxy. With Voltaire, the "scientism" of the eighteenth century had settled in deeply, and the natural law that Voltaire defended had much more of the character of Lockean empiricism than of traditional natural law within it. To be sure, it was an ostensibly humanistic social physics that Voltaire spoke of so glowingly, and its immediate political bearing was clearly intended to be left of center in its direction.

Nonetheless, if epistemology is a better test of ideology than is substance, the drift of natural law could not have been made clearer than by what Voltaire did to it. His quest for certainty was real, and it was untempered either by a bounded relativity or by the strains of a less precise or earlier rationalism. It was, rather, truly representative of the views of the new nominalists, with an angry Voltaire once telling the German ruler Frederick the Great, "metaphysics, in my opinion, is made up of two things, the first what all men of good sense know, the second what they will never know. . . . We are equipped to calculate, weigh, measure, and observe; that is natural philosophy; almost all the rest is chimera."[4]

With Voltaire, what had remained as a kind of naturalness within the Thomist view of law was certainly well diluted by the end of the eighteenth century. Yet Voltaire's calculus of law still contrasted sharply with what happened to the natural law across the Channel under the stewardship of Sir William Blackstone. Blackstone, of course, was more purely a legal scholar than Voltaire, but he nonetheless molded the final stage of eighteenth-century natural law into something that satisfied the demands of counterrevolutionary political thought. Blackstone made sure that his jurisprudence was based upon an epistemological foundation that could support it against the "proud reason" of the Enlightenment, but he did so because he, like Voltaire, aspired to a high level of stability and predictability within the law. His belief in the reasonableness of the English common law buoyed his contention that the common law and the natural law had merged into a fortuitous hybrid that could instruct Englishmen in everything from their metaphysics to their daily legal principles. Yet Blackstone's sense of "reason" is closer to what most would understand as the process of human reason*ing,* and it is far different indeed from what the early natural law prescribed. More than likely, it was the muted tone of the common law judgments, ostensibly filling the logical gaps of yet untried legal fact situations, or perhaps it was the commercial nature of much of the common law's substance that facilitated the dominance of the internal calculus within that law. Yet, for whatever reason, the availability of the common law melded so well with Blackstone's purpose that Blackstonian natural law mimicked the "science" of the eighteenth century, while at the same time it preserved the commonality and the utility of a routine and ostensibly logical legal decision.

The modern struggle between faith and reason, as it turned out, was most convenient for Blackstone, for he was able to plead that his system of laws was based upon values and that, in a typically naturalistic fashion, the mechanics of his system only linked morality and the law more firmly. How closely, incidentally, that same argument was to be to that of Adam Smith who, within economics, argued for a linkage of a real-world market valuation and a natural notion of what value and price should be. Of course, the linkage between these two elements under Blackstone (and Smith) was ultimately dubious, the linkage being one of sequence and logical form rather than one of pure integration of method. Yet the general principles of Blackstonian morality, we must remember, were never held to be inherent but were, instead, both derived from, and reliant upon, a mechanistic logic. At one time, such devices staved off the more egalitarian and organic pleas of the Enlightenment while they possessed the sanctity of both faith and reason. The epistemological straddling and the resulting ossification of the law that resulted from it is well described in Daniel Boorstin's *The Mysterious Science of the Law,* yet the writings of Blackstone, along with Voltaire, still represent a clinging commitment to a latter-day notion of natural law. With this, we need to look now at what was left of nonempirical legal rationalism at the turn of the nineteenth century.[5]

The German Phoenix

Legal richness comes from many places, and all legal systems have their wellsprings. The English had cases. The French had their *Institutes,* and the Germans had within their nationalistic spirit what most of the nineteenth century did not give them in reality: a political state. The roots of historicism were made up of anything but the Teutonic rigidity that English and French scholars have often derided it for being. Early German romanticism, of which historicism is a first cousin, was largely a rejection of form, an attempt both to find a national heritage and to reject the intellectual domination of the all-too-didactic Enlightenment. Frederick von Savigny, the German legal historicist, said it well: "the historical spirit . . . is the only protection against a species of self-delusion, which is ever and anon reviving in particular men, as well as in whole nations and ages; namely, the holding that which is peculiar to ourselves to be common to human nature in general."[6]

Savigny's perception symbolizes the contrast between latter-day rationalism and early romanticism. Ernest Barker's introduction to Otto Von Gierke's *Natural Law* makes it clear that the German school is a rebellion against the natural law, but Barker sees this positioning as "a reaction against its [the natural law's] rationalism, against its universalism, and against its individualism."[7] His point is a crucial one, and particularly with regard to universalism and individualism, it is the tone of the latter-day didactic natural law that Barker is objecting to rather than the substance of either a more comprehensive natural law or a specific early view of natural law. It is, in other words, both the brazenness and the brittleness of late-eighteenth-century law—the threat, or indeed perhaps the eventual reality, of a tyranny descended from a presupposition of a discovered order—that impelled the historical school to rebel. Roscoe Pound, in his *Legal History,* sensed this when he argued that historicism was a "reaction from two phases of the natural law thinking in its last stage, namely from the paper-constitution making . . . and from the belief in the power of reason to work miracles in legislation and consequent no less confident code-making of the end of the eighteenth and beginning of the nineteenth century."[8]

Historicism was, in short, a rejection of the "legislative theory of the law-of-nature school in a period of legislation and codification with which the reign of philosophy came to an end."[9] Clearly, the historical movement within Germany, in a flavor reminiscent of the early German economic historicists such as Bruno Hildebrand and Karl Knies, incidentally, did represent an attempt to rescue the more or less nonempirical side of law from the clutches of both Voltairian and Blackstonian rigidity and Revolutionary overbearing. Savigny embraced a portion of a traditional view of natural law when he argued that "in times past, with the omission of certain prominent peculiarities, a natural law was formed out of the *Institutes* which was looked upon as the immediate emanation of reason."[10] But Savigny describes this rigid process "with pity" and then attacks those "who hold their juridical notions and opinions to be the offspring of pure reason, for no earthly reason but because they are ignorant of their origin."[11] For Savigny, it was thus only the "historical sense" that, as he put it, "protect[s] us against this, to *turn upon ourselves* is indeed the most difficult of applications."[12]

Even into the late nineteenth century, the historicism of G. F. Puchta still reflected an internal and even somewhat relativistic quality within German jurisprudence. Puchta pointed out that "the share which Usage has in connection with the origination of this form of Right [customary right] is frequently represented so that Right is said to arise out of Custom, an opinion which agrees with the materialistic notions already mentioned."[13] But Puchta believed the very opposite to be true, or that "usage is only the last fact of the process, by which the Right, which has arisen and is living in the members of the people, completely externalizes and embodies itself."[14] In brief, Puchta rejects anti-Hegelian materialistic epistemologies and their preference for externalities, arguing instead for a law wherein "the consequence of this [his own] mode of origination, induces a diversity of Right among the people."[15] This position signifies a recognition of a fundamental differentiation, almost a relativism, among peoples and their law. It also demonstrates a preference for an internal- and essence-derived notion of the very origin of law. Puchta's relativism is honed from a distinction among nationalities and not among personalities, but Puchta still recognized a fundamental relativism in the law.

For Rudolf Stammler, writing in the early twentieth century, there was an opportunity for another attempt to retain a legal suppleness through the use of a customary law. His law, rather than being "a question of 'expediency,'" was still a product of a "folk spirit" and a "recognition of [a] fundamental conception of law and national life as a whole."[16] Stammler was concerned with maintaining the "Romantic Conception," as he called it, which he believed had "disappeared earlier in all other fields of learning" but that had "maintained itself longest . . . in jurisprudence."[17] Stammler rebelled against attempts "to still one's philosophic conscience," and he argued that the desire "of modern jurisprudence to go as far as possible in the generalization of concrete legal material" had created a situation that "overlooked the fact that one must necessarily distinguish between *pure forms of conceiving and judging* and the *material* treated according to those forms."[18] Stammler, at the time of full maturity of German romanticism, believed that the attempt to "supplant juristic philosophy" with a more concrete notion of law violated something that he found essential to a flexible conception of that law.

Psychologically, there can be little doubt that the German historical school of jurisprudence clearly signaled the first attempt to recapture and preserve the "soft" half of the earlier natural law. The attempt to fill the abandoned portion of the old rationalist view was not only an early example of a naturally left-of-center predisposition in the law; it was an espousal of a view that eschewed mechanistic rationalism at the same time that it maintained the breadth of an experience of a people. Hegel might have chided Savigny for the intellectual sparseness of his historicism, but notions about the law were not so far from what Savigny was up to. Hegel himself, and here A. P. d'Entreves in his widely read piece on natural law is probably mistaken, was very much the embodiment and not the rejection of both reason in the law and of the human progress that the Enlightenment had ostensibly stood for. Within the larger debates over the law, Hegel stood clearly on the side of higher law in its confrontations with positive law, for Hegel insisted that a society's rules must be a reflection of the truth and the rationality of that polity's moral principles. This linkage with moral principle is paramount within the Hegelian mode, and in contrast to Kant's concern with the internal or logical consistency of the law itself, Hegel is concerned that the law reflect the essentials of those fundamentally different components of life that exist outside law's formalities.

I shall say more about Hegel and his views on the law shortly, but for now, let me observe that Hegel is well within the tradition of the soft side of an earlier and more psychologically neutral natural law. His linkage of law with morality, the human order, and the order of the universe, along with his belief in the interlocking nature of the relationship of one citizen's will with another's, is very much a counterpoise to Kant's more clearly "contiguous" understanding of human existence and legal order.

Kant and the Will

If by the close of the nineteenth century we can already see a major division within the precepts of natural law, we should also, on the other side of the metaethical division, be able to trace the other separation on the road to modern legal positivism. The denial of any element of inherency within the law is at least as old as Creon in Sophocles' *Antigone,* but in the modern period it is Thomas Hobbes who initiates the positivist separation from traditional natural law. Hobbes supplanted the natural law with the imperative mode, and, in addition to subverting the questions of morality and value within the law, his imperative view insisted upon both a logical efficacy and a functioning order within the law. Robert Kocourek, in his discussion of the general dominance of the imperative school, said that "the law, considered as a whole, has always put more emphasis on order, certainty, and regularity than on the elusive idea of justice."[19] He suggests further that though "our law moves on a road of natural law . . . in practice, it moves on the wheels of expediency."[20]

Thus, Hobbes, the great purveyor of both internal order and expediency, is the originator of the antinaturalist or skeptical position in early legal thought, and his conventional and regulated form of law carries itself, with increasing psychological bias, right through Kant, Bentham, and eventually Austin. Again, the imperative school, along with its analytic and positivistic successors, is one half of the skeptical position within the larger metaethical division and, as Heinrich Rommen puts it, those that have historically opposed the positions of natural law have won out largely because "the idea of natural law obtains general acceptance only in the periods when metaphysics, queen of the sciences, is dominant. It recedes, or suffers an eclipse," he argues, "when being . . . and oughtness, morality and law, are separated, when the essence of things and their ontological order are viewed as unknowable."[21] It is not surprising that Thomas S. K. Scott-Craig, in his review of Locke and natural right, finds that Locke was never truly able to respond effectively to the legal absolutism of Hobbes. To a degree, of course, the reason for that is that Locke, like Hobbes, was interested in the "orderly mechanical behavior of solid atoms"; therefore, the choice for epistemological mechanism and ethical individualism, even at Locke's stage of the dialogue, easily triumphed over the value-oriented notions of internal essence.[22]

The Lockean tradition of ethical individualism, particularly as it was sometimes expressed through the notion of the "will," was surely continued by Kant, for Kant was concerned that the law not only be free of any notion of innate value but also be a succinct and pristine whole unto itself. "I have made completeness my chief aim," Kant says in the *Critique of Pure Reason,* as he sought a system of jurisprudence that was both comprehensive and self-contained.[23] For Kant, in other words, personal rights are as much a matter of contract as, for example, the contractual alienation of property is argued to be a uniting of two wills. Such separatism, of course, also demonstrates the influence of Pufendorf on Kant as well as Locke, for not unlike Locke who was weaned from his naturalism by mechanistic contract notions, the skeptical Kant was easily influenced by a form of separatist mechanics that was itself based upon a mathematical or internal calculus.

Kant's notions about the origin of the law are also significant. I do not agree with d'Entreves that Kant was "the most forceful exponent of natural law theory in modern days when he maintained that the practicing jurist should turn 'to pure reason for the source of his judgments in order to provide a foundation for all possible legislation.' "[24] Yet d'Entreves is correct when he argues that Kant's criticism of legal empiricism is such that one can never know what the law is "but only what *pertains* to the law."[25] The confusion stems from the fact that there is, of course, a kind of rationality to the Kantian notion of law, but it is the rationality of *application* and application *within* the law, for, again, we are speaking of the internal consistency of law, not of its validity. The key concern for Kant was always the internal consistency of law, not the truth of the law. He was also concerned with the imperative nature of both the law's being and its enforcement. Such concerns took precedence over both the *verum* of the law and its links with the essence of a human order or a human morality. Though d'Entreves's point that "Kant's doctrine of the 'autonomy of the will' is usually taken to mark the end of the natural law tradition" is essentially accurate, it is also indicative of Kant's dedication to the removal of the need for moral investigation or for the "overlapping" or associative notion of the interests or moral thrust of a polity's members.[26]

Thus, the interdependence of empiricism, formalism, and legal universality in the imperative notion of law become apparent not only logically but psychologically with the evolution of the imperative mode. The deemphasis of morality restricts the considerations of the law to the continually "interactive" conditions of society as opposed to internal or associative conditions. The distinction between God's law or even the secular natural law after Grotius's revisions, on the one hand, and the man-made or imperative law revisions, on the other, is more clearly possible with this kind of understanding. As d'Entreves correctly points out, the writings of both Aquinas and Hooker had well recognized the vastly different charges of the two spheres of law.[27] The Kantian insistence on the dominance of man-made law, again, insures that only the contigual, bordered touching, or the external conditions of the atomized citizen, are the legitimate concern of the law.

Of course, this latter point is really quite obvious once the psychology of it is understood, for the matter of contigual fit is very much where we have been before. The questions of morality, or even of "God's law," involve something very personal, and the study of the human essence is in close psychological affinity to the concepts of joint, associative or overlapping considerations of personal morality and law. The Kantian "cleansing" of the law, the psychological setting of line to line with exactitude, is significant not only for reasons of its disregard of morality; it is even more important because of the potency of the configurational structure that it imposes upon the entire discussion. The only result of the imposition is legal formalism, and the Kantian formalisms were, indeed, the very notions that led to the abstractions, the universalisms, and the "general law of jurisprudence" that the analytic school has trooped across the legal stage.

D'Entreves accents the parallel birth of the historical interpretation of law and of modern, positive jurisprudence.[28] He misses the mark. The very priming of the formalist arguments that accompanied the analytic school were clearly moving toward a psychological purity, while on their side the historicists were left with using their original psychological predispositions to at least remain aware (as d'Entreves admits) of the dual "political" and "technical" life of the law. As we have seen, d'Entreves argues that "theirs [the historicists] was at bottom a 'dualist' theory; they never accepted the fundamental assumption in Hegel's legal philosophy that the ideal finds its revelation in history."[29] Yet, I must disagree again. The *ideal* may have found its *revelation* only in history, but it found its intellectual fulfillment in the dialectic, which, as a matter of course, also allowed for the future inclusion of newer and different kinds of considerations. In short, if anything was dualistic, it was Hegel's view of the law, a point that, I believe, brings us back to the Boorstin recognition of the stultifying coalescence of the Blackstonian interpretation of natural law and the common law and the arresting of law's growth that occurred on the rationally crystallized side. The historicist view and the Hegelian view were very different from the Blackstonian/Voltairian view and the Kantian notions of the law, as well as from the later Benthamite brand of utilitarianism.

Bentham and Austin

Armed with a mechanistic view of the law and armed as well with a political impetus derived from an essentially negative view of freedom, the Benthamite utility theorists now did to the law what they had to leave to the next generation in the field of economics. The minimal differences between Kant and Bentham, as in the retribution/utility argument within the criminal law, have been vastly overstated, even if only for the reason that the attributed rationality and responsibility of the offender in both cases is quite similar. To be sure, Bentham introduced his thinking about the law within a context of "the general inclinations of men."[30] He also attacked the latter-day fixations of the didactic natural law when he charged that its supporters have written as though "there had been a real code of natural laws."[31]

But Bentham, in a sense, was guilty of much of what he accused Blackstone of, for the foundation of his own edifice was made up of the calculus of pleasure and pain. In a manner that would have made Voltaire proud, Bentham provided for the calculus's application to legislation by simply confining the concept of public good to an understanding of the science of positive legislation that science consisted principally of knowing what was good.

In a general sense, the Benthamite tradition, with its ironic criticisms of Blackstonian natural law, has continued to carry the legal day, particularly in the English-speaking world. John Austin, representing the full flowering of the analytic school, was a descendant of Bentham, serving a personal tutelage under the utilitarian master. Austin barely conceded the existence of some form of a "general jurisprudence" but rejected the inherent nature of law except as it came from an abstraction of the commonalities of various positive laws. For Austin, like his predecessors, the origins of the evaluative process could never be considered a priori or as a function of reason. They can claim their verifiability only as they manifest a product of contemporary usage.

As Austin himself wrote, "with the goodness or badness of laws . . . it [the law] has no immediate concern."[32] It has, instead, only a "consideration of utility," and when it is there, "it adverts to such consideration [only] for the purpose of explaining such principles, and not for the purpose of determining their worth."[33] Austinian formalism, of course, led to the sanctification of both immediate legal usage and legislative or judicial origins of such usage. Predictably, it led back to a modern reverence for the political state in a way that Hobbes had only spoken of as an ideal. The political dominance of a threateningly chaotic world fit well with what the new randomist/skepticist, empiricist/rationalist coalition eventually did for the philosophy of law. Can there be any question that this process is so very close psychologically to the Voltairian and Blackstonian pruning of the natural law and its richness on the other side of the division?

The Other Side of Skepticism

The psychological coalescence on the other side of skepticism allows for the understanding of a different derivative from legal skepticism. That other side of skepticism, which ironically is often referred to as neo-Kantianism, is prominent in Western law, and it is found in the writings of figures like Hans Kelsen. Such neo-Kantianism is very different from the metaphysical neo-Kantianism of Schopenhauer and Nietzsche in at least one sense, because it does, quite simply, move the other way, or to the left on the psychopolitical continuum. Kelsen is an important figure in the development of modern law, for amid what appears to be an attempt at the creation of an elaborate internal logic for the law, Kelsen inevitably found the more generalized notions of legal authority coming into play. Kelsen's search for law's broader justification resulted in his *Grundnorm,* the allegedly immutable foundation from which law grows. That *Grundnorm* led Kelsen to sources like written constitutions, but Kelsen always seemed to find that he could not stop there. The real *Grundnorm* was to be the highest form, the last regress in the analysis, yet even there

Kelsen could not overcome having the fundamental rule be derived and not inherent.[34]

If Kelsen represents the turn away from the most rigid of the analytics, it is H. L. A. Hart who has more recently reached over still further and introduced the one side of the "analytic" or skeptical position to a suppleness if not an outright relativity within the law. This movement began with Hart's central distinction between primary and secondary law, the former being a more internal notion or a more or less universal acceptance of socially understood norms as a bedrock for legality. Hart agrees that these primary norms are often understood as custom, but he does not prefer to use that term himself because, as he notes, "it often implies that the customary rules are very old and supported with less social pressure than other rules."[35] Nonetheless, there are, according to Hart, primary nonlegislated or adjudicated understandings and these, rather than the formalized laws of a society, are the best evidence of what Hart describes as "an essential point of contact" between human morality and the law.[36]

Clearly, Hart is rejecting the position of the more purely analytical view, for though he would go along with the notion of the law's essentially analytic nature, he does not fully accept the Austinian notions that view law principally as the command of a sovereign. Law, for Hart, did not have to be an imperative or a command. Indeed, he found these descriptions to be what he called "threadbare" explanations for the law. Further, in what appears to be an acceptance of an essence within the law that is larger than the Hobbesian notion of law's enforceability, Hart demands that law comply with notions of a regularized and equitable procedure.

Just as important, Hart argues with equal vigor that the imperative theory is that the very concept of "command" itself is far too vertical. It is based upon what he calls a "simple relationship of the commander to the commanded, of superior to inferior, of top to bottom; [that is,] the relationship is vertical between the commander or authors of the law conceived."[37] In Hart's discussion, he describes different types of legal rules, but he differentiates between commands that import verticality or those that might exist within the criminal law on the one hand and those that he claims preserve the freedom of "individuals to create structures of rights and duties for the conduct of life" on the other.[38] For Hart, these latter kinds of rules provide "faculties for the realization of wishes and dreams."[39] They do not, necessarily, import a linkage with any notion of natural law, but they do rather clearly portend an affinity for personal voluntarism and at least a tacit linkage between private "wishes" and the possible harmony among private wishes. This voluntarism is particularly significant when it is echoed by Hart's "internal" definition of the primary laws, for Hart's acceptance of those personal wishes parallels the acceptance of the very consideration of what people believed that the law ought to be doing.

Interestingly, Hart's succeeding point in his article on law and morality deals with the penumbras of the law, but rather disappointingly, Hart does not recognize that the gray areas of the law are at least in part a product of the "ought" or, better, of the "oughts" of the morality/law connection. Hart's penumbras, rather, investigate the law's incompleteness, or the cracks between the clearer holdings of law. What would have happened if Hart had seen that there is another kind of penumbra within the law, and that it comes through a relativism among the plural "oughts"? Still, Hart clearly criticizes the modern procedure of "deciding cases in an automatic and mechanical way,"[40] and his movement toward a "soft" or a rationalist/relativist position within the law is apparent again by the nature of his attack upon the natural law itself. Hart chastises natural law as being "in all its portean guises" made up of more "attempts to push the argument much further and to assert that human beings are equally devoted to and united in their conception of aims."[41] Again, I must note how close to, and yet how far that understanding is from the mark, particularly since Hart's own work sought a pluralistic or aggregated notion of the law. The position of Professor Hart in the famous Hart-Devlin debates over homosexuality was such a clear argument for an expansion of the permissible *range* of human conduct, and though this argument for an increased range may well be one of the principal derivatives of legal relativism, Hart felt that in order to favor an expanded range, he had to divorce law from morality. He should have done the exact opposite, that is, once he had taken what was in effect a protorelativist view along with a left-of-center substantive position, he should have *rejoined* law with morality (moralities) and enhanced the permissible range through the acknowledgment of these multiplicities.

Again, overall, it is difficult to be very critical of Hart; he signals, without question, a firm positioning on that behalf of the nexus between supple rationalism and bounded relativism that the left coalition has been approaching. Given his legal heritage, his views are advanced, and they in fact do represent that portion of the soft or relativistic coalescence that comes from the skeptical side.

Functionalism: The Second Phoenix

If the German historicists signaled the first attempt at rescuing supple rationalism in the law after Blackstone, Voltaire, and the legislationists pulled it apart, it was the functionalists, along with their first cousins, the legal realists, who made up the latter-day Anglo-American and French attempt at a restoration of legal subtlety. By the turn of the twentieth century, at the time of Roscoe Pound and Léon Duguit, this second attempt at a kind of quasinaturalism was determined to link itself with moral, political, economic, and other considerations in order to find a broader equilibrium of justice within the law. This attempt grew primarily from a conscious recognition of the differences in man's interests or, as Duguit once said, from man's "different aptitudes and diverse needs."[42] Pound, the American, referred to the common law as being "made up of compromises of conflicting individual interests in which we turn to some social interest, frequently under the name of public policy, to determine the limits of a reasonable adjustment."[43] Pound wished to accomplish such compromises by concentrating on "legal claims by which within certain limits such interests are legally secured."[44]

At another level, Pound sought a clearer definition of those social interests, which in turn permitted what he called the equitable "weighing" of various "interested" claims. Clearly, though Pound was not at the point of a value relativism, his recognition of the legal impact of acknowledged multiple social and ultimately legal interests sought to refute the formalism and universalism of the earlier perversions of natural law. Referring first to the eighteenth century and the deducing of natural rights from "some metaphysically given fundamental formula of justice," Pound railed against those like Herbert Spencer, who "as late as 1891" tried to enforce "a scheme of individual natural rights deduced from a formula of equal freedom"[45] Pound likened such a scheme to a jurist's "deducing individual, public and social interests respectively by a logical method," and he made it clear that he would have no part of these "necessary presuppositions of law."[46] Indeed, he described such institutions as "schemes of observed elements in actual legal systems . . . reduced to their lowest terms and deduced *ex post facto*."[47]

Duguit and the Continent

The preference for a modern organic relationship between law and the needs of industrial society were, if anything, even stronger on the Continent where Pound's thinking was mirrored by Léon Duguit. Duguit rejected the individualistic notion of man apart from his polity and attacked both the substance of Lockean rights and the method of Lockean formalism at the same time. Duguit's allegiance to a notion of organic solidarity was an attempt at the formation of a new social norm, a human *méson* that was to grow out of the diversity of human society. Duguit persisted in declaring that this *méson* was not a part of any natural law, saying that his norms, rather, make up "a rule of law not because there is a superior principle . . . but because there is a rule which has penetrated the consciousness of men living in the same social group who understand."[48] Yet such a position stands both as something close to natural law and as evidence of a fear of a philosophy that was torn between an empirical strait jacket and its own potential rebirth as the vanguard of antianalytic law. Duguit's response avoided the nineteenth-century disrepute of natural law by focusing on both "social norms" and the solidarity of a populace. It also, however, represented a belief in a deeper linkage between human "interests" and moralities within the law and the "spontaneous production" of the law itself. To be sure, the functionalists' concern with group interests, or even the realists' preoccupation with the ideological immediacy of judicial decision making, was still a good way from relativism, but, again, the attentions of the functionalists to the questions of social equity, within a framework that transcended the logic of the law, clearly made this second brush with psychological coalescence both a bolder and a more successful effort. The result was not a new natural law, but it was a prototype of what a relativistic natural law might become. In short, it was an overture to human inherency and morality, and it was decidedly favorable in its coloration toward the ideological left.

What the historicists had only salvaged from the natural law the functionalists were beginning to reconstruct, and in the shadow of the larger metaethical and now legal realignment, the appearance of a modern, more ideologically focused depiction of natural law was rather clearly foretold.

A Different Natural Law

It is difficult to say precisely when the new natural law fully returned. Nonetheless, if not with Gierke then certainly with Lon Fuller, there was a clear recognition of not only a desire to reconstruct something that would resemble traditional natural law but also of a need to find a much clearer understanding of what went awry originally. Fuller specifically cites the damage that Hobbes's linkage of a judicial decree to the will of the sovereign had caused, scoring Hobbes's plea in the *Leviathan* for a return to things natural as being nothing more than a polite and "escapist" tribute to traditional philosophy.[49]

Also, Fuller is critical of modern antinaturalism, scoring Kelsen's "methodological premise," even with its welcome candor, as being too mechanistic and much too representative of a "faithful adherence to a consciously imposed limitation of method."[50] In his discussion of the law of property, Fuller suggests that "we would encounter much that was founded on reason, but we would also discover that, like all human creations, this institution has its arbitrary qualities, [or] its sharp corners that violate the fluid contours of nature."[51] In a discussion of Oliver Wendell Holmes and legal predictability, Fuller subtly realigns both legal concepts and legal technique toward a position of duality, claiming that terms such as "control," "tort," "title," and the like are only "ambiguous in the sense that they have two distinct meanings and each of them stands for a relationship that can be viewed from two quite different sides."[52] The "under" side, as Fuller called it, helps us to "find compelling reasons for the things that are done by the courts in cases where these are used," and the "upper" side merely presents "the action of the court as a brute fact divorced from the reasons that gave rise to it."[53]

Notice that with this dichotomy too, Fuller, like Hart with the analytics, has intentionally avoided resolving the tension between the substance and the reasoning, or between the essence and the method, of the law. His attack on Kelsen's mechanism is thus at the same time something more and something less than a simple broadside; it is a conscious attempt at a *broadening* of the law. From it we can begin to detect the ephemeral outlines of the permanent tension that is so necessary for the substance and the method of legal relativism. Such a position is surely expansive methodologically, but it is also, quite obviously, left of center as well. In this sense, Fuller is indeed close to Hart's attempt to legitimize a left morality outside of traditional social and legal norms, and yet Fuller recognizes that the need for the "oughts" within such social and legal norms is the essence of the law's vitality.

Fuller's condemnation of positivism's justification for majority rule of law—that is, that something is law "not because it is right but because it is most likely to be obeyed"[54]—is not quite the same as his perception of Austin's and Kelsen's "never let[ting] the green fields of life lure them from the gray path of logic" in law.[55] Yet, there is no doubt that in Fuller's eyes these two positions have a very real linkage, which I submit is ultimately psychological. As Fuller says, the legal method, if it be the scientific method of positivism, will always enforce "a substantial taboo against any intelligent discussion of the vague and shifting forces which ultimately shape men's lives."[56] Further, the arguments for a formal law take law and "freeze it into rigidity" and eliminate what Fuller states is "the plain fact that ideas are capable of growth."[57] Incredibly, in the very mentioning of both the law's capacity and its need for growth, Fuller adds wistfully that "if one wishes to be mystical one may describe this process in Hegelian terms as the dialectic of history."[58] How better to have put it? The process of growth in the law is indeed very Hegelian, and I would argue that such an understanding places Fuller right at the other side of the drawbridge, just across from H. L. A. Hart and from where the new rationalist/relativist coalescence begins within the law.

Let us not forget that Fuller had a lengthy, wonderfully civil debate with Hart on the issues of positivism, naturalism, and the law. Fuller, though guilty in that discussion of an unfortunate confusion when he argued that the internal coherence of the law is better when law is good than when it is evil, still demonstrates a deep ideological affinity with Hart by agreeing that Hart's preference for procedure as the underpinning of law is close to his own emphasis upon "fidelity" to the law. In a sense, the "procedural" hand of Hart that Fuller perceives is extended to meet the "fidelity" hand of Fuller, and though the linkage based upon the acceptance of faithful procedure may ultimately promote only a single morality, the gentle Hart-Fuller debate illustrates well the rising intellectual and ideological affinity of the opposing logical schools.[59]

In retrospect, the most remarkable thing about Fuller may still be that he was willing to argue so vigorously for the natural law at all. From Fuller's writings, the qualities of (a) an aversion to legal mechanics, (b) the presence of an epistemological linkage of a humanistic morality with the law, and most important (c) the creation of a unique dualistic tension between the form and the substance of law attest to what a revived view of naturalism in law should represent. It was a worthy pathbreaking effort, and it was one that had significant followers in other places, particularly on the Continent, where the Frenchman Francois Gény mirrored many of Fuller's views. Gény, in questioning the mechanical applications of law every bit as vigorously as Fuller, even criticized the common law as being a false formula for the reasoning out of current cases. Gény argued that courts and judges should be able "to recognize that procedures and their applications must be controlled by the discretional evaluation of the one interpreter who alone is able to adapt to concrete facts."[60] No judge, according to Gény, must decide cases in an atmosphere in which the judge sees himself as apart from his polity, and no statute, as he put it, must be "applied with the preconceived purpose of restricting its scope."[61] According to Gény, the better road for justice can come only from a "restoring [of] the communication between legal reality and jurisprudence."[62]

Arthur Harding, in his article on the revived natural law, says about Gény that he "does not try to . . . formulate detailed principles of law by any process of logical deduction."[63] What he does, according to Harding, is point out that "human law will take its form through the interaction of certain sociological factors including the facts of environment, the tradition and habits of people, [and] the standards of conduct generally conducted by the people."[64] Harding's commentary on Gény and the natural law is significant, for Harding adjudges the revival of natural law to be a signal of man's "participation by reason in the divine plan of the universe."[65] More significantly, he sees it as a denial of the human ability to supply "all knowledge or . . . detailed rules of conduct."[66] For Harding, man's best hope is to have a "compass" within him, a compass that Harding argues permits a "latitude for variation and deviations in human conduct."[67] In a beautiful depiction of a softly rationalistic and nearly relativistic view, Harding reminds us that St. Thomas did not return man to absolute reason, for he believed that man "can never encompass or discover the absolute; [but] that he can approximate it, moving closer as his power and faculties are increased."[68] What, after all, could be more representative of either the thinking of Hegel or of the psychological left?

Obviously, my own views are partial to Fuller, Gény, Harding, and the others who have revived the robust and humanistic side of natural law. Their thinking demonstrates a clear psychological sensitivity to the need for the broadest ranges in the law and for a watchfulness concerning the crystallization or hardening of legal principle. Their method or, better, their antimethod is clear, and it serves us well in maintaining the breadth of what may be called protolegal considerations in the law. Also, it calls for the full inclusion, as Hegel also insisted upon, of the losing as well as the winning interest in the realm from which the law takes its substance. What we ought to be able to see now is that as political ideologies become more representative of psychological predispositions, which they are doing, the impact of codified law will be similarly more psychological. The kinds of tensions within the law that draw upon such subjective orientations will never be "resolved," and thus the law will do well to maintain the tension in a "looser" and less crystallized condition.

Hegel understood this tension as it existed among the perceptions of law, particularly as he accepted the tension between the *verum* and the *certum* of law. Now, as we cross into that kind of conflict more deeply, we should see that if Hart, for example, had been ready to accept the range he argued for as coming from the disparate, that is, the plural, moralities of humankind rather than from an absence of morality, as he chose to do, and if Fuller had only sensed what was causing the ambivalences that he found within his revived natural law, their discussion might have arrived at a relativistic nexus under its own power. Of course, the very existence of these differentiated moralities is increasingly the result of different human psychologies. Yet the understanding of what encompasses at least a substantial part of the looseness within the contemporary concept of natural law could extend Hart's range at the two poles (or bordering penumbras) of the ideological spectrum and include predispositions toward law as they flourish within different personalities' perceptions. Such a process neither perverts nor destabilizes the law but only recognizes that law, like reason, is itself an aggregate and that the most relativistic view of law provides for the largest range of acceptable behavior.

The Recent Record

Unfortunately, the near rapprochement of Professors Hart and Fuller has not been understood, much less continued, by their intellectual successors at Harvard and Oxford, Professors John Rawls and Ronald Dworkin, respectively. Without time for a full review, let me merely point out that the Rawlsian "original position," with its required "veil of ignorance," clearly violates the Hegelian requirement of consciousness about the law.[69] Rawls, in his *Theory of Justice,* goes so far as to argue that a citizenry should not only not know of their respective economic positions but, indeed, that it should not know "their conception of the good or their special psychological propensities" as well.[70] He does this, ostensibly, to limit the demands upon law to those of primary social goods, something that he hopes will "avoid introducing . . . any controversial elements."[71] The "autonomy" that this will provide comes, as we would expect, from a central Kantian assumption that ethics and therefore law must be both generalizable and universal. Rawls, who speaks so endearingly of justice, makes it clear that justice "does not assume that the parties have particular ends, but only that they desire certain primary goods."[72] In turn, these primary goods are reasonably "derived, then, from only the most general assumptions about rationality," and permit us not to worry about "whatever in particular our aims are."[73] Rawls, I am certain in good faith, respresents this "theory" as a left-of-center position in law.

At Oxford, Ronald Dworkin, though ostensibly extending the scope of individual rights and liberties, seems oblivious to either the intellectual history or the current directions of left-of-center thought. Dworkin vigorously distinguishes his "principles" for their ability to secure "some individual or group right" from the "policy" that advances "some collective goal of the community as a whole."[74] Instead of recognizing a complementarity within a collectivity's goals, in great part because he is unwilling to deal with bias in any meaningful way, Dworkin argues that decisions as odious as the nineteenth-century enforcement of the fellow-servant doctrine were accomplished without regard to the relationship of the worker and the entrepreneur. In fact, in discussing debates over morality, politics, and the like, Dworkin argues that "it is wrong to suppose that reflective citizens, in such debates, are simply setting their personal convictions against the convictions of others."[75] In the operation of law, it is clear that Dworkin has no concept of either legal heterogeneity or the aggregation of values that comes with legal relativism.

Legal relativism and the legal theory of the Natural Left has thus unfortunately advanced little beyond Hart and Fuller; perhaps only one writer, Richard Wasserstrom, seems to be searching for ways to adjudge the law and the rights that live within it in a manner that is capable, as he says, of "comparing and weighing capabilities for measuring" such rights.[76] Wasserstrom realizes how difficult it is to gauge "interpersonal comparisons," surrendering to the task by saying that the values he speaks of are either "equal for all persons, or if there are differences, they are not in principle discoverable or measurable."[77] Well, what if they are discoverable? What if they are measurable? Perhaps, if they are, we can resume the search for legal relativity, although we now need to move on to economics.

Economics

Although the impact of the metaethical division within various fields is slightly different, there are striking parallels across the disciplines of social science. Economics, though a separate intellectual pursuit for far less time than either law or philosophy, still demonstrates what in the contemporary era is the psychological interface between metaphysical questions and the questions of its own discipline. Without question, the modern econometric model is the furthest extension of economic positivism, and the arguments within the economic community and among those who study economics generally reflect the same psychological continuum that we have seen elsewhere.

The Physiocrats began modern economics, yet their varied and sometimes obscure prescriptions oftentimes bespoke social and even ethical perspectives more than economic admonitions. Their affinity for a pastoral and generally nonmaterial existence was certainly traditional in a logical sense, but to classify any single figure along a psychological continuum, whether Francois Quesnay, Anne Robert Jacques Turgot, Pierre Samuel Du Pont, or the rest, is difficult enough, and to classify the group is simply not possible. Certainly, there were strains of epistemological skepticism in the work of these preclassicists, a reaction, perhaps, to the emerging laws of mercantilism and free trade.

The definitions of history, however, cut more sharply than those of its watchers, and the classical school of economics reveals a more decided tilt in a psychological direction than did the Physiocrats. The modern market, in its way, became the economic analogue to the Voltairian legislationist technique in eighteenth-century law, for it promised a rationalization of a unitary notion of value as it placed the value question itself into a method and withdrew it from metaphysics altogether. The classical assurance that "natural price," "natural value," and the like would be reflected fairly within a market's mechanism is not so different from the Blackstonian merger of natural and common law of the same period, and it is notable that the psychological division among the early economic rationalists begins at much the same time that the legal historicists sensed that the cutting edge of legal rationalism was getting a bit too fine.

To be sure, Ricardo's laws of rent and wages attempted to save early classicism from its drift to the right, and his concept of "labor embodied" still stands as a hallmark of the holistic determination of a worker's worth. Yet labor embodied had to contend early on with Malthus's "labor commanded," which, in its way, was an early confirmation of the market's dictates, even when the perils of the iron law of wages were well understood. Later, Say's Law, with its presumed confluence of demand and investment, further justified the modern apparatus and extended into macroeconomics the ostensibly reassuring equilibriums of working capital. It may be fair to say that by the time of a full-blown utilitarianism in law as well as in economics, the analytic side of rationalism had completed its fission from the less didactic rationalists and was more than prepared to fuse with the utilitarian skeptics, who were already inclined to a more precise form of economic analysis.

Thus, in economics, perhaps even more than in law, the merging of utilitarianism with overordered rationalism was accomplished with considerable ease. Maybe the ease of it was due to the fact that the utilitarians, principally Bentham, did not intrude upon such a long tradition of rationalism in economics as they did with the natural law. Alternatively, the very nature of economics may have accelerated its early adaptation to mathematics; perhaps the entire subject is more fungible than even the common law's mercantile-oriented writs and judgments could ever be. Nonetheless, we know that the utilitarian strain begins with Locke, a rationalist in law as most would see it, and yet a thinker whose extensions through Hume and Bentham make the transition to a logically skeptical view even more facile in economics than in law. Hume's epistemology avoided rationalism and left a priori or inherent notions of ethical value at the same place that economic notions of inherent value soon stood with utilitarian economics.

Jeremy Bentham, of course, solidified the utilitarian calculus within economics, and his consequent economic justifications for things like the enclosures earned him the wrath of economic historicists like Sir Henry Maine. Maine, who is best known for his depiction of modern history as a movement from status to contract and who illustrates the position of a latter-day skeptical relativist reasonably well, was ostracized by the utilitarians in economics, principally because of the epistemological breadth that his largely historicist viewpoint insisted upon. Yet Maine's depiction of Bentham as one who justified the economic grievances that he ostensibly opposed politically further illustrates the narrowness of the burgeoning utilitarian method in economics.[78] Of course, fundamental to this utilitarian mode was the abandonment of the assumption of that natural harmony of human interests that Smith spoke of so fondly. At one level, the search for equilibriums within economics—something that became central to the later utility efforts—was the very catalyst for the rejection of the idea of larger social harmonies. If the little pieces could be made to fit edge to edge, then the grander and more heterogeneous pieces, it seemed, could be largely ignored.

Such a position, of course, not only obscured the questions of value and inherency within economics but also continued, much as Maine sensed, to ignore the larger questions relating to economic as opposed to noneconomic contributions within society. Again, this divorcing of the economic enterprise from social, cultural, and ethical concerns, like the acceptance of utilitarianism itself, could occur both earlier and more completely than a similar separation could with law. Economics was determined to be a "science," as free of values as it was "value," and not even the conflict of different kinds of interests, as the functionalists could argue for in law, would fit within the emerging calculi of latter-day utilitarianism. Bentham is traditionally referred to as a philosophical radical, but the term defies a psychological perspective. His philosophical commitment to a solitary notion of humanity and his rejection of pure laissez-faire analysis is derived, not from more modern democratic political notions, but from a Hobbesian view of the necessary state role in the diffusion of incipient human conflict. Like the Austinian legal notions of sovereignty that soon followed, Bentham asks for an economic guidepost to which economics can repair within a modern society. As a result, his philosophic and economic views are close to those of the more nihilistic skeptics, and they are clearly the work of a conservative psychology.

The Road Back—Mill

On the traditional rational side, Ricardo evidenced the first attempt at rescuing humanity from rationalism. But another figure, John Stuart Mill, represents the last great English attempt at a reconciliation of economic perspectives. His work illustrates the near impossibility of a left-of-center perspective's rising above the tide of a discipline's biases without a conscious appreciation of psychology. The case of Mill is a tragic one. Without question, the great burden of his work was to overthrow the method that his father and his father's friend, Bentham, imposed upon him in his early years.

His great economic work, *The Principles of Political Economy*, came out in seven editions, beginning in 1848 and ending in 1871, and if there was ever a clear transition within a major intellectual statement it is Mill's metamorphosis from a sterile early utilitarianism to what many have called the near socialism of the 1871 edition. Clearly, the traumas of Mill's personal life and the dominant conservative themes within contemporary economics slowly pulled Mill's natural sensitivities into his work. Yet, what is equally clear is that Mill, for all his transcendence, still furthered what Robert Cumming called the final separation of logic from psychology in British political philosophy.[79] Instead of adopting an economic theory based upon human nature, Mill unfortunately fell prey to a perspective that allegedly maintained psychologically neutral logic within its treatments of moral and political issues. Though disturbed by the inordinate economic distributions that early capitalism generated and though unwilling to accept the explanations and justifications of his contemporary economists, Mill acceded to the critical methodological credo of the more ordered classicists by repeatedly separating political economy from deeper metaphysical questions. At one point, Mill admitted that "I do not attempt to decompose . . . mental operations . . . into their ultimate elements," and he even suggested that most of his conclusions "have no necessary connexion with any particular views respecting the ulterior analysis, i.e. . . . 'the science which deals with the constitution of the human faculties.' "[80]

Thus, the last liberal nineteenth-century gasp of redistribution economics succumbs to a severance of the very question from higher quandaries, much as the later editions of Blackstone increasingly are read to forestall the raising of questions of legal justice. The lines of intellectual separation match the psychological lines of those who draw them, and Mill, unfortunately, defaults in his opportunity to rejoin and reconsider the distribution question anew. Almost predictably, Mill, in his later writings, turned increasingly to a "poetic vision" of the world as he realized more fully that Bentham's mind and the calculus of utilitarianism were not "representative of human nature."[81] He saw that his childhood teacher created philosophy out of "minds like his own" and was given, ironically, to ignore things like "psychological facts [and] complex forms of sympathy."[82] To be sure, there is a faint glimpse of different kinds of human minds here, and in a most revealing phrase Mill chastises those traditional scholars who have "busied themselves for two thousand years, more or less, about the few universal laws of nature [and] have strangely neglected the diversities."[83] Yet how unfortunate it is that Mill's latter-day pondering about a "superior comprehensiveness" of method within philosophy did not minister to both his early separation of political economy from philosophy and the separation of philosophy from psychology. During the nineteenth century, there may have been no firm perception of relativism, but surely Mill's own recognition that a quest for what he called a "higher conformity to the universal requirements of human nature," in spite of what he saw as the "diversities of human nature," might have forestalled the surrender of an increasingly ordered rationalism to the awaiting utilitarian linkage.[84] In his reflections on his own earlier works, he saw himself as a "dry, hard, logical machine," and he realized that he had never seen the difference between "merely having feeling" and "being conscious of this feeling."[85]

We may ask whether an economics that had come from something other than a "logical machine" or an economics that reflected a consciousness of feeling would have prevented the easy linkage of economic rationalism and the utility side of skepticism. But, in their failure, it was not long before early classicism, under the tutelage of writers like Jean Baptiste Say, was to meld economic classicism to the utility school. The elements of automaticity are not difficult to find in Say's insistence on the linkage of investment and demand. His notions of human economic maximization surely would conflict as well with Mill's later years' notions of human asceticism. Indeed, such assumptions fit so well within the emerging marginal utility school that classicism is, by the time of the work of the Austrians, almost indistinguishable from the economics that was blossoming on the logical division's other side.

The Emerging Left

Before we discuss modern utility and neoclassicism, we should recognize that beyond Mill's thrashings within classicism there are two economic schools that come along in the nineteenth century and more clearly light the way to the emerging, if tardy, reconciliation of soft rationalism and relativistic skepticism within economics. The first, of course, is socialism, with its principal proponent being the Frenchman Jean Charles Simonde, better known as de Sismondi. Let us not forget that the socialist reaction to early capitalism was in part a commentary upon law, a reflection of a feeling that the natural law could be radical as well as conservative.[86] The modern notions of freedom, equality, and justice could be drawn from the great principles as much as from a formula for economic expansion and early socialists like Henri de Saint-Simon, Robert Owen, and Charles Fourier all held utopian notions of the perfect society.

De Sismondi, however, is the more orthodox socialist, and his work reveals the first early touches of psychological coalescence. As Eric Roll, the economic historian, remarks, there is a "great deal of Sismondi which is romantic," and indeed there was a skepticism there, a suspicion about the promises of classicism's perfect order.[87] Romanticism had freely embraced "its lack of logic and its scorn for rational comprehension," and though it drew on traditional mercantilism and cameralism for its purely economic theory, its basic thrust was "opposed to the philosophy of natural law and its utilitarian development."[88] The very progress of Sismondi's work shows an evolution from classicism to a romantic, or logically skeptical, socialism. Indeed, his first major work, published in 1803, is the work of a pure free trader and capitalist, and by 1819, in *Nouveaux Principles,* he is most critical of the classical method, the effects of capitalism on human welfare, and the very idea that there is a natural harmony within capitalism.[89]

What socialism was to the early part of the nineteenth century, historicism was to the middle of the century. Clearly influenced by the legal historicism of Savigny, German historicists like Wilhelm Roscher also reflected the anti-individualist philosophical underpinnings of continental romanticism. Roscher's *Grundrisse* was an organic rejection of economic classicism, and it was significant both in the development of the social reform movement in the United States and England as well as in the work of latter-day historicists like Hildebrand and Knies. Hildebrand's writings signify a clear rejection of the classical school's claim for the discovery of natural economic laws, while Knies's later and more radical work argues for a full separation from the classical method, claiming that it could never yield what the physical sciences were said to be able to do.[90]

Thus, with classical socialism and German historicism, the subtly rationalist and the subtly skeptical positions do demonstrate the early fission from the more dogmatic classicism and the utilitarian skepticism that they each abhorred. Economic historicism, much influenced by legal historicism, fell to the same fate of its forerunner and did not effectively survive the nineteenth century. Socialism, though more virulent and long-lasting, was soon captured either by those like Auguste Blanqui who were themselves more radical socialists or by Marx who, as we shall examine later, also forestalled psychological reconciliation within economic thought. Nonetheless, the early dominance of conservative economics should not be understood as being solely the fault of the fledgling left-of-center perspectives. Something else was happening in the latter part of the nineteenth century, and the full flowering of the utility school did more to assure the dominance of orthodox economics than did either the virility of classicism or the impotence of either socialism or historicism.

The Utility Revolution

With the ascendance of the utility school, the skepticism of Hume and Bentham in its more pristine forms finally achieved dominance within the discipline of economics. The Malthusian criticisms of David Ricardo and the impact of Say's fixation on the economic transaction both opened the door to the three principal utility theorists—William Jevons, Karl Menger, and Léon Walrus—and assured control of economic orthodoxy for the formal and psychologically external brand of economics. The notion of marginal utility was not brand new, but under the guidance of Jevons, the concentration upon the exchange of goods, services, or whatever was made complete; thus, according to later commentators like Joseph Schumpeter, economics could now come home from the naturalist detour of Smith, Ricardo, and Mill.[91] Though formal utility theory was not adopted by governments until the economic crisis of the 1930s, its intellectual merger with the more structured rationalists signaled the certain end of the logical division of schools within economics and fully enshrined the concept of maximizing the individual and the economic transaction. What was now left was for the modern macroeconomist to embrace the assumptions of that maximizing citizen and understood his transactions within the larger economic community. This means that by the end of the nineteenth century the sway of the new classicist/utility alliance was so strong that even those of subtle disposition who sought to flesh out economics into broader equilibriums were caught in the epistemological web.

Alfred Marshall was extraordinarily innovative in his explanations of demand elasticity, consumer surplus, and producer surplus; yet his major contribution, as Keynes later stated, was the "grafting to the long-term equilibrium ideas the marginal principle of substitution, together with some discussion of the passage from one long-period equilibirium to another."[92] Marshall was later criticized for the highly simplistic assumptions of his work, but he himself wanted to return to a softer classicism and tried to update the work of Ricardo and Mill by attempting to weigh the value of the entire human product into value kinds of considerations. Nonetheless, the quality of value in the *Principles* (1890) is still very much a matter of cost and utility, and Marshall's discussion of value still lacks what Richard Meek called either "social or productive considerations."[93]

The Burden of Keynes

If Marshall's attempts at a return to a softer notion of valuation fell to the onslaught of margin and exchange, what happened to perhaps the greatest of the twentieth-century economists is even more indicative of the psychologically conservative rationalist/skepticist coalition in economics. If John Maynard Keynes wished to be known for one quality of his life's work in economics, it was that the element of certainty held no place in the new science. Substantial and important matters have been too easily forgotten about the early Keynes, and the most considerable of these is that Keynes' early career had little to do with economics. Keynes was originally concerned with probability theory, and his roots in the modern kind of relativistic skepticism are clear in his extraordinary work on the difference between risk and uncertainty. Keynes was thoroughly aware, as Ray Harrod, his biographer, once observed, that "no knowledge acquired by inductive reasoning reaches the level of absolute certainty." More important, Keynes also understood that "probability is relative in a sense to the principles of human reason."[94] He went on to say that "the degree of probability . . . does not presume perfect logical insight, and is relative in part to the secondary propositions we in fact know."[95] The short of it is, as the economist James Cochrane well understood, that probability is never a logical phenomenon in any Bernoullian sense, and Keynes clearly understood that this was so as well.[96]

Again, the Keynesianism that followed Keynes, in great part because of the overordered perversions of John R. Hicks, always claimed more certainty than Keynes would ever have allowed. It is Cochrane again who points out that the ability to compare marginal, valuational, and capital kinds of quantities is possible on a personal level but never on a logical level. As Cochrane says, Keynes' discussion of probability "was centered on just this logical impossibility of a one-dimensional comparison of multi-dimensional relations."[97] Keynes and his prescriptions for depressed economies are frequently cited as being the saviors of the economic system, capitalism, which Keynes quite thoroughly despised. But it is probably just as appropriate to cite Keynes' work as one more unwilling ratification of the latter-day conservative coalition of hard classicism and utility theory. Both as a rescuer of theory and as a rescuer of the liberal states, Keynes was never able to sense the need either for a different epistemological foundation or for a different psychological bearing.

The Modern Confrontation

In great part because of the failings that we have highlighted in these last pages, the epistemological biases of formal economics have become quite pronounced. Without question, the hard classical/utility skepticist position is the dominant economic mode, and a few among current practicing economists even seek to challenge it. The work of Joan Robinson and Pierro Sraffa has questioned the dominant mode from the perspective of imperfect competition very well. Yet, as Sidney Weintraub has pointed out, the momentary emphasis on "non-competitive price formation, uncertainty, externality and public goods" often revert to a mere "re-examination of the micro-foundations of macroeconomic theory" and "the continued study by mathematical economists of the theory of n-person games."[98]

Again, what is lost sight of by all but a few is that the linkage with the emerging coalition that led to modern monetarism and the mathematical economists was born of the metaethical shift and the accompanying epistemological biases. A recent article by Thomas Mayer cites the deep debt to Hume that monetarism possesses, Mayer claiming that of the twelve characteristics of monetarism, five are explicit, two implicit, and that the "preference for stable money growth fits the whole tenor of Hume's discussion."[99] Perhaps the fullest recognition to date of the coalition of the psychologically conservative skeptics and classicists comes from a recent article by Richard McKenzie that, without acknowledging any psychological underpinning, still argues that there has been a partial reconciliation of the neoclassical and the Austrian economic views. Curiously,

McKenzie sees neoclassicism as "positing a fundamental distinction and conflict between the internal subjective world of the individual and the external objective world in which the individual pursues his goals."[100] McKenzie is convincing when he cites the epistemological and methodological link of Milton Friedman's major essay on the methodology of positive economics with Paul Feyerabend's equally distinctive attack upon positivism in an article that is subtitled "Outline of an Anarchistic Theory of Knowledge." McKenzie acknowledges that a strain of Austrian subjectivism, or what he properly calls a "radical subjectivist" view, has it that "people buy things for various reasons and the things they do buy, although appearing to be the same thing, are actually quite different."[101] The heart of the Austrian position, McKenzie argues, is close to conservative neoclassicism, with a "Lockean style social contract" notion being represented by such writers as the conservative Robert Nozick.[102]

The Psychological Variable

Yet, whereas McKenzie is not quite ready to place psychology at the core of the epistemological debate, one recent article appearing in the *Journal of Social Sciences* at least acknowledges the possibility of the psychological underpinning of the entire argument. Daniel Fusfeld draws attention to the period of Keynesianism, recognized also by Eric Roll in his history, when there was a feeling that a reconciliation of the major groups in economic thought had been achieved. There was, to use Fusfeld's phrase, a "lull in the usual methodological disputes," but since that time, it is clear to Fusfeld that "new epistemological and conceptual issues have arisen that challenge the scientific claims of logical empiricism, general equilibirum theory and mathematical models."[103] What is so important about Fusfeld's article is that he explicitly argues that it is "psychology [that] contributes broader and more complex foundations for an understanding of behavior than the economists' assumptions of utilitarian optimizing."[104] In other words, just when Roll, the Keynesians, and even Paul Samuelson thought that there was an emerging "grand neoclassical synthesis," a new recognition has now dawned on at least some economists that, to use Fusfeld's words again, "some people were able to perceive and understand larger and more complex patterns than were others."[105]

What we are seeing here, I will argue, is a hint of relativism at last, but in its explicit form it has taken until now to appear, and that is why the orthodoxy of economics still reigns so powerfully. To be sure, the psychology of the countermovement to orthodoxy was just below the surface over the last few years. Sherman Krupp had said that the "scope" of economics was the real problem with the discipline and that it was a problem that required the understanding of "new conditions or new variables." Krupp argued that conventional economic theories do not "apply to conditions of high uncertainty or rapidly changing tastes, nor can they cover situations where choices tend to be noncomparable."[106] Jerome Rothenberg had specifically argued that modern attempts at a restoration of value theory were easily thwarted because "the values which form the central subject matter of value theory are objective" and are therefore only falsely "interpersonally comparable."[107]

G. L. S. Schackle, long a critic of modern economics, had reminded us that "economics is only one color in the spectrum of those [human] affairs in their general totality,"[108] and Lawrence Nabors has noted that what economics has all too long set out to do is to "work out the details of a set of propositions which are independent of the political, social and psychological predispositions of their authors."[109]

The psychology of it, in short, has been coming along, and the latter-day antipositivists have been beginning to sense the need for a broader epistemological base for economics. We need, of course, to go beyond a simple broadening of the argument or beyond epistemological neutrality. We need, I think, to recognize that, just as Leonard Silk criticizes giving the 1974 Nobel economics award to both Gunnar Myrdal and Friedrich von Hayek as "really nothing more than a false and passive neutrality," an active search for a truly relativistic model of economics is now in order.[110] The illusion of the neutrality of logic is the heart of the difficulty with utility in the first place, and James Buchanan, a radical economist, is correct in challenging the *psychologist* to provide us with a "better explanatory hypothesis."[111]

Both Buchanan and Jerome Rothenberg, another left-of-center economist, are correct in recognizing that the new commitments in economics must come from psychology; but Rothenberg, as have so many others, stops himself too quickly when he argues that it is difficult in such a search to obtain "one's own consistent relative evaluation" of economic value.[112] What if Rothenberg, like Wasserstrom in the law, found the core of the differentiated human valuations? What if, as Fusfeld now argues, "a firm foundation for scientific economics [has] at last been achieved"?[113] Perhaps if, after all, the psychology that Fusfeld speaks of when he argues that "psychology contributes broader and more complex foundations for an understanding of behavior than the economists' assumptions"[114] is the relativistic psychology that we are beginning to understand, then the theoretical notions of relativity may be ready to take hold. We have waited a long while for this to happen, and orthodox economics has exacted a great price in the interim. Let us now look at sociology and anthropology.

Sociology and Anthropology

The two deeply interrelated social science fields of sociology and anthropology cast a somewhat different shadow over the epistemological sorting out of the psychological right and left. Two principal reasons account for this, the first being the rather late arrival of these disciplines to the intellectual arena, and the second being the largely residual nature of the subject matter that each discusses. On the first point, Peter Ekeh reminds us that most major strains of modern thought were well developed by the time of sociology's introduction.[115] On the second, as one anthropologist put it to me with mild overstatement, "it's a discipline without a subject matter."[116]

Though both of these factors somewhat complicate an analysis of the psychological shakeout, the second is perhaps the more confounding. Philosophy, jurisprudence, and even economic theory were present at the heart of the fission-fusion process, but sociology and anthropology evidence fewer roots that trace back to early rationalism or skepticism. Some commentators, like Thomas Kuhn, say that sociology and perhaps anthropology are still in preparadigmatic periods, but unquestionably Weber, Durkheim, and Simmel, along with latter-day figures like Parsons, Gouldner, and Lévi-Strauss have still contributed significantly to sociological understanding.[117]

Though the content of much of early sociology was frequently holistic, the epistemology of early sociology tended toward formalism, a product perhaps of things like the Weberian citizen-felt duty to fill the gap of professional regularity left by the decline of the Junkers. Rousseau, Alexis de Tocqueville, and even Marx might have surrounded the Comtian origins of sociology with a variety of different perspectives, but modern sociology truly begins with Max Weber who, apart from his attempt to provide for a professional bureaucratic elite, also sought to respond to the radical sociology of Marx.

Weber himself drew a good deal from both German romanticism and historicism, but the recognitions of subjectivity that that kind of antirational skepticism often imported were usually well braced by Weber's need for sound empiricism. The acknowledgment of consciousness, *Verstehen,* almost motivated its own triumph over perceptual unclarity, and the fact/value distinction, in large part, were Weber's cure for excessive subjectivity. As Anthony Giddens points out, Weber specifically eschewed "psychological teleology," reserving it for the description of specific unique events, as for example the impact of Frederick William IV's personality upon his actions and history generally.[118]

Beyond fact value, of course, the Weberian contribution was the ideal type, a search for a rational model that abstracted the concrete events and modes of reality into a theoretical purity. To be sure, Weber did argue for the observation of more than "methodological postulates," but his preference for the pure type was closely linked to a sense that free private action was the closest to rationality, and therefore the operation of ideal institutions was closest to the truly rational order of the world.[119] Again, though Weber's roots were sufficiently German to include Savigny's notions of evolutionary law along with the collectivity and personality emphasis of Georg Von Below, the search for purity of the abstract model indicates Weber's leaning toward the conservative side of that skepticism, reaching over to the more empirical rationalists.

To be sure, as Werner Cahnman points out, Weber acknowledged two different kinds of evidence, one being rational-mathematical and the other being of an emotional or artistic nature. Yet, as Cahnman notes, Weber "recovers his positivistic posture immediately" and places "rational social action" at the heart of what he searches for.[120] Within his economic viewpoint, this bias has meant that Weber maintained a strict institutional loyalty to formal economics, among other formalisms, even when he was not in full agreement with the human nature assumptions of the new Austrian marginalists. As Cahnman points out again, Weber had a sense that Roscher, Gustav von Schmoller, and others of the historical school were correct in their criticisms of Menger, particularly with regard to the "one-sided assumptions" of self-interest that Menger's view represented.[121] Yet, in *Economics and Society,* Weber reasserted his primary interest in what direction human action would take "if it were strictly purposive-rationally oriented, undisturbed by error or emotions and if, furthermore, it were unambiguously oriented toward one single, especially an economic purpose."[122]

Weber, of course, was only one of the three great early sociologists. Georg Simmel's background was altogether different from Weber's, and his intellectual style differed greatly as well. Simmel too was of a logically skeptical orientation; but, perhaps in reaction to the rightward movement of so much of skepticism under Weber and the neo-Kantians, Simmel evoked an almost Hegelian set of notions of social groupings and sociology. Simmel's cognitive style has been called "insightful rather than expository" and "digressive rather than systematic."[123] More important, the essence of Simmel's belief centered around an evolutionary or a "becoming" notion of human existence. Culture, though important, was secondary for Simmel to a human existence that would create and enjoy cultural objects as well as subjectively experience them in various ways. Further, Simmel maintained the tensions of several intellectual dichotomies, seeing life not only as a "flux and becoming" but also as a "livid but not known" entity.[124] Further, the tensions between the one and the many, between our life and our work, again in Hegelian fashion, were held to be all a part of some reconciliation, something that Simmel addressed when he said simply that "life is one."[125] Surely, such a view represents a reaching for the soft rationalist and vaguely skeptical side of what little of the logical division extended into sociology.

As the early German sociologists were at least largely the descendants of logical skepticism through historicism and romanticism, the French, and particularly Émile Durkheim, were more the product of the early rationalism of France and England. Durkheim himself was clearly influenced by Comte and studied Spencer extensively as well. Durkheim is known for his development of the idea of a collective consciousness, and, with the overlay of the kinds of biological models that came from Spencer, he sought after the cardinal rules of the human collectivity. Yet, in a curious and psychologically conservative manner, Durkheim argued that we could not "infer social laws from biological laws," and in his attention to what he hoped would be an autonomous and highly specialized science of sociology, he went on to argue that the collective conscience would have to be gleaned from singular collective expressions in law, art, and other social products. He even argued that statistical averages should be used to determine a kind of social mean in these intellectual areas.[126]

There is little question, then, that Durkheim's conservatism engendered a rejection of the human range or relativity, something that he further demonstrated by his firm rejection of human consciousness. Curiously, even within his discussion of human anomie and particularly within the discussions of suicide that Durkheim is so noted for, the French sociologist once again declined to deal with subjective states, insisting instead upon an objective determination of social "health" as opposed to social "disease."[127] His concern with human health, however, was nothing that would permit either introspection or subjective reflection, and his notions of social function, correspondingly, were both mechanistic and atomistic. The result of these positions was that function itself was held never to be related to individual aims or to any form of singular human causation but were held, instead, to be entirely a product of "preceding social facts."[128] Here again, as with so many of the psychological conservatives, the strain of intellectual progress is perceived as stemming only from the taughtly drawn confines of a single discipline at the same time as the relationships within the discipline are perceived only as being a part of a logical calculus.

Thus, even in a brief review of the three principal figures of classical sociology, not only do the psychological predispositions of these writers shine through rather clearly, but the beginnings of the movement from the logical to a more psychological standard begin to shine through as well. With more contemporary writers, the presence of the psychological bearing is clearer still.

The Reach to the Left: Dahrendorf

Ralf Dahrendorf, writing in the mid-twentieth century, is one contemporary sociologist who has lent a keen psychological insight to his work.

Dahrendorf, unlike many sociologists, had a strong sense of the role of the early intellectual schools; in an essay entitled "In Praise of Thrasymachus," Dahrendorf's attack on modern-day positivism returns to the logically based roots of early political and social thought.[129] While routinely ascribing both authoritarianism and the origination of individualistic liberal thinking to Hobbes and also seeing Rousseau as a theorist of both democracy and collective totalitarianism, Dahrendorf argues for the general notion that all vertically structured power is inherently corrupt. Most significantly, however, Dahrendorf cites Thrasymachus's choice of argument with Socrates as particularly laudable, though the early Sophist chose to demand "a clear and concise statement" on Socrates' notion of authority.[130] I would argue that Thrasymachus's standing as a logically left-of-center rejecter of authority may not have made the Sophist as psychologically left of center as Dahrendorf wanted him. Yet, it is nonetheless clear that Dahrendorf is not only convinced of Thrasymachus's orientation but that Dahrendorf himself is at least reaching for a psychological kind of analysis. Unfortunately, his own statement against positivism is ironic in view of his quotation of Thrasymachus, for Dahrendorf argues that "refinement is not necessarily a sign of truth."[131]

In short, Dahrendorf's own prescription, if not his historical perception, is more clearly of the anticonservative psychological view than are the views of earlier left-of-center sociology. Dahrendorf's preference for a theory based upon equilibrium (though he presents some awkward examples in law and politics) is still an attempt at something that is "much closer to the richness and color of events" than something "scientific."[132] Further, though he deals with power rather more favorably than many on the true psychological left would, he clearly sees the evolution of power or the "permanently changing outcomes of the dialectic of power and resistance" as something worthwhile.[133] Such an impatience with false stability, along with a quest for a broader social homeostasis, is typical of Dahrendorf's work, and his "Out of Utopia" criticizes a major contemporary like Talcott Parsons for creating a structural functionalism that Dahrendorf sees as "essentially something self-sufficient, internally consistent, and closed to the outside."[134] Dahrendorf, though perhaps a bit unfair in his characterizing of Parsons in this manner, is deeply opposed to the notion of a separated and internally logical strategy for sociology, and Dahrendorf even carried that view into a criticism of Robert Merton, whom Dahrendorf saw as arguing for a separation of theory and research. Dahrendorf also noted that "the advocates of empirical research and abstract theory seem to get on quite well" with comparatively little "friction and controversy"; at the same time, he saw that excessive empiricism and abstraction was greatly responsible for the frequent irrelevance of his discipline.[135] "How is it possible," he pondered, "that sociologists, of all people, should have lost touch with actual social problems and questions of which there are so many in the world?"[136] Indeed, Dahrendorf even suggests that sociologists have, if anything, contributed to "the trend toward conservatism that is so powerful with the intellectual world today."[137]

Again, my own view of Dahrendorf's work is that it still reveals a good deal of the logical rather than the psychological left. Yet, not unlike H. L. A. Hart, who also began with logically skeptical origins, there is a clear sense of where it is that Dahrendorf would like to go. Further, there is a sense that, in spite of the antirationalism of his favorable commentary on Thrasymachus, Dahrendorf is reaching over toward the soft side of rationalism in his attempt to give a normative direction to sociology as a discipline.

The Parsons Controversy

Let us move on now to Talcott Parsons. Certainly, no figure in contemporary sociology is so discussed and so criticized as is this prolific modern writer. Traditional sociologists have found him difficult and obscure, and other sociologists who have presumed to speak for the left, particularly the Marxists, have reacted sharply to his openly anti-Marxist view. My own feeling is that Parsons is a good deal more on the psychological left than his detractors would like to concede: though he is superficially identified with his sociological structural functionalism, even his early work evidences a clear preference for the study of actions of individuals and their purposive origins. Parsons, we must remember, was critical of Weber for attempting to explain so much of sociology "without general concepts and without a 'nomological' knowledge or general theory."[138] At the same time, Parsons himself was careful that his own general concepts were not crystalline abstractions but were, instead, attempts at emphasizing "the cultural, the symbolic and the subjective." They were clearly attempts to go beyond the ideal types that Parsons argues never told one how they "are combined, fit together one with the other, etc."[139]

At one point, Parsons specifically noted that ideal types would exclude "certain possibilities of variation on other levels"; as one of his biographers, Hans Adriaansens, notes, Parsons wanted "the fixed relations within the 'ideal type' [to be] broken open and laid bare to analysis."[140] Parsons was, of course, nothing if not ambitious. He renounced Merton's apology that the best sociology could do was midrange theory and reached openly for a grand theory of his own.[141] In part, the placement of Parsons on the relative and softly rational side of the new psychological division is a reflection of Parsons's general denunciation of narrow, analytic models within all fields, including particularly those of orthodox economics. Parsons attacked the reification of theories that did not, as a minimum, include deviance along with conformity and the general along with the analytic.[142]

At another level, the suppleness of Parsons's position on both grand theory and epistemology is accompanied by clear references concerning the importance of human psychology itself. Parsons wanted, as he stated, a theory that would include "the subjective and particular aspects of [an] actor's orientation," and he saw the trend of modern behaviorism as denying the search for the internal or innate purposes of human motivation.[143] He wanted a kind of voluntarism that combined not only objectivist with subjectivist positions but that also complemented the social-nominalist position with a social-realistic perception as well. His general denunciation of utilitarianism and his perceiving it as within the province of the exterior, the post hoc, and the domain of the all-too-rational "efficiency" and "technical rationality" are psychologically significant as well.[144] Again, Parsons's voluntarism represented a dogged attempt at reincluding the subjective into what he correctly perceived to be an increasingly positivistic sociological science. With the retrospection that will come with the psychological perspective, I think that Parsons will be viewed as representing an important step toward an antipositivist left within sociology.

The New Left

Perhaps no one attacked Marxian sociology with greater vigor than did Talcott Parsons. What is interesting, however, is that during the period of the New Left Parsons was attacked for his alleged conservatism by many who, though logically left, revealed epistemological preferences that were, if anything, well to the right of Parsons. Once again, the rotation of the metaethical axis was not bringing a simultaneous confluence of psychological positions to the left and right. The neo-Marxists of the New Left, of course, thought of themselves as the true left, and though the continuing rotation did bring about a sometimes more significantly psychological left, it was too often tied to traditional positions on the left that were anything but psychologically radical.

Possibly the clearest representation of such a position, and a view that does include a thorough chastisement of positivism, is Alvin Gouldner's 1970 work, *The Coming Crisis of Western Sociology*.[145] Gouldner's orientation is apparent from the outset, for within a quest for a relevant and involved sociology, Gouldner nonetheless wishes deeply for a clear and objective science of sociology to emerge.[146] Gouldner is doggedly existential in his formulation of how this clarity is to be accomplished, and, in a manner consistent with his quest for objectivity, he says that he does not wish to "psychologize social theory" for that would, according to Gouldner, "remove it from the larger social system."[147]

To be fair, Gouldner does correctly sense much of what has happened to traditional sociology. He recognizes that the utility notions that came from Saint-Simon through Parsons and Merton did work toward an understanding of the human collective and that some of sociology was concerned with the whole of society in a supple and synthetic way. But Gouldner's toughest critique is saved for a condemnation of the early rather than the late positivism, an emphasis that is ironic in view of Gouldner's own rigidities. It is true, as Gouldner suggests, that after the fall of the Napoleonic order in Europe and during the "clash of right against right, Positivism affirmed the propriety of an amoral response to the social world."[148] Also, that period did develop an "amoral method for making maps into a moral rule."[149] Gouldner recognizes that after Saint-Simon there were two broad sociological groups, one leading from Barthélemy Enfantin and Saint-Amand Bazard to Hegel and Marx, with such early romantics as the two former figures fully embued with an "appreciation for the role of hypothesis, intuition and 'genesis' in the process of knowing."[150] The other group, that of "Academic Sociology," was more the Comtian faction, and it—as I think Gouldner correctly understands—

became less concerned with substance and more obsessed with method.[151] Thus, sociology, which was emerging from a time of loss in belief, did go through the beginnings of fusion of the psychological styles, and there is no question that the "non-calculating, moral utilitarianism" of Marx did join the conflict between utilitarianism and some notion of natural right at the same time that it evidenced an early stage in the development of a psychological left.[152] Nonetheless, though it was a softer science than what we often see in modern positivism, Marx did conclude by arguing for a scientific socialism, one so rigid that Gouldner feels the need to cite both Antonio Gramsci and Georg Lukács as softeners of what came from it.

Modern positivism, as we know, came along full tilt after the Marxist period, and it is clear that functionalism, in that late-nineteenth-century period, did serve as an academic apology for new power relationships, new economic arrangements, and the ever rising middle class. Yet what is not so clear is that functionalism was inclined to spin off only to the right in any psychological sense under the tutelage of those, like George Homans, who later encased the moral social arrangements in theories like those of social exchange. Indeed, the original combination of functionalism and voluntarism was somewhat left of center psychologically, it being in a sense an attempt to return to a social utilitarianism. Gouldner is correct in saying that, with the advent of Spencerian positivism and Skinnerian behaviorism, the seeds of conservatism were certainly sown. Yet Gouldner is unhappy with the style of Parsons's and others' rejection of that conservative sway. Indeed, Gouldner reveals his own psychological bent quite openly when in commending Parsons's functionalism over Durkheim's he does so for reasons that are centrifugal and not centripetal. As he said, under Parsons man is not a part of the "collective conscience and exoteric social currents."[153]

Again, Gouldner reveals his own predisposition more than anything about Parsons, for in identifying Parsons with social values and with humankind as an entirety, he decries the acceptance of institutionalism as a resignation to order at all costs. I find Gouldner's argument rather perplexing, in part because of my feeling that the absence of some idea of functionalism has been as individualistically chaotic and thus conservative in the Hobbesian sense as institutionalism has been when it is overbearing. What perplexes me more greatly, however, is that even Gouldner concedes that there is an opening to what he calls a "left-Parsonianism" in all this, particularly with the writings of Neil Smelser and the dynamic open-ended or change-embracing notions that are found there.[154] In fact, for an instant Gouldner seems to perceive such an open-ended functionalism as being almost neo-Marxian, embracing many of the sources of change beyond economics. Yet, in the final analysis, Gouldner still concludes that functionalism cannot truly adapt to change, and Gouldner thus falls well short of the psychological left.[155]

Unfortunately, as Gouldner concedes, the New Left was itself still "too young to have produced its social theory"; and even Gouldner's instincts, though often accompanied by calls for a self-consciousness about where we are going, are still largely prepsychological and reflect a great deal of logically randomist skepticism about the social order.[156] The result, though hardly conservative ideologically, is, again, not left in any psychological sense. Gouldner's work stands as a reminder that as late as 1970 the fusion of soft rationalism and bounded skepticism in sociology was still undone.

Recent Developments

In the years since Gouldner, only a little has changed. Perhaps, however, some of it is worth noting, for though it is clothed all too deeply in existential thought, there may be a somewhat clearer understanding today of both an epistemological as well as a valuational range of positions within sociology. Richard H. Brown represents these insights when he transcends a logical separation such as that between the Cartesian "speculative mathematical, logical-deductive tradition" and the Baconian, "empirical, inductive, research-and-fact oriented" view and argues that both perspectives are ultimately deterministic.[157] Brown is correct in his perception of neopositivism, seeing that its laws of probability, disproof, and falsifiability are somehow cleaner than early positivism, and he cites Karl Popper's notion of the piles of a pier being driven into a swamp and connecting with nothing real as being an inappropriate response to neopositivism.[158] Popper's wish, according to Brown, is only to make positivism workable, and Brown claims that the humanist critique is very different indeed in its requirement that we know the "reasons for meaningfully intended conduct."[159] In short, Brown looks forward to a kind of rejection of positivism that opposes both the Kantian (hard skeptical) pregiven categories of understanding and the Comtian (hard rational) world of concrete facts. Though Brown is not able to make the leap into a recognition of psychological bias, and though he places a bit too much emphasis on process or "the norms and rules of inquiry itself," it is clear that Brown's 1977 work is moving toward a better psychological understanding of fundamental dichotomies.[160]

One more recent sociological piece that leads in the correct direction is a work by the Norwegian, Dag Østerberg, which argues against behaviorism from a dualist perspective, contending that the logic of nature and the logic of sociology are not the same and therefore should not undergo the same kinds of explanation. "Physics is about matter," he argues, and goes on to say that society is different from physics because "society is the totality of all social phenomena."[161] For Østerberg, "the way of the world is, therefore, a synthesis of natural processes and social processes."[162] There is a nice balance in that kind of statement, a subtlety that is accompanied by Østerberg's specific endorsement of ambiguity as a source for the flow of history and as a process that leads to greater understanding.[163] It is a Hegelian vision, of course, and Østerberg recognizes this himself when he cites the importance of the behavior/action dialectic and argues that experiencing actions gives us a "[s]olidarity with Others that makes it possible to discover strangers."[164] With a nice touch, Østerberg suggests that "the fact of becoming a stranger is to become acquainted with something or someone else," and therefore, the "main theme of sociology" should be to study our "mutual, dialectic relationship to each other."[165]

Surely this is heady stuff for sociology, but just as surely, it is more clearly of the psychological left than almost anything sociology has seen so far. Once more, Østerberg says, "the most important thing here is the fact that the encounter with the Other has provided one with an outside and with that, also an inside."[166] It is a beautiful statement, and it presents a duality that, in true Hegelian form, is on the lip of reconciliation, teetering toward the monism of Hegel's unity of opposites. Østerberg may see only that it is supported by the duality within us or "by the dialectic unit between intention and action,"[167] and he may see only that such a dialectic opposes "pseudo-mutual dialectics," which, like a machine, are characterized by "the fact that it periodically repeats one or a series of movements."[168] But, again, the duality is near its unity, and the divisions of the dialectic are beginning to fall to the reconciliation of complementarity. Once more, I find Østerberg, Brown, and a few others—criticizers of the positivism of hard skepticism and hard rationalism—to have moved the left-of-center fusion of sociology as far as it has gone to date. A full reconciliation under psychology is not evident, however, and, as a consequence, the conservatives are well ahead on the other side of the chasm. Yet the hope for sociology is real, partly because of the nature of its subject, but perhaps more specifically because it is presently nearer the leap away from epistemological rigidity that the Natural Left requires than jurisprudence, economic theory, and perhaps even philosophy. In short, there seems to be a clearer sense of the spirit of both the dialectic and human relativism here than there has been in other places; and, to return to an old theme, we seem to be closer to a fundamental break in epistemological modification within sociology, particularly within the shift of the monist/dualist dichotomy, than we are in almost any other discipline.

The Better Vision: Anthropology

I say almost because, again to return to old themes, there is a discipline, albeit a small one within the vastness of social science, that seems to have had a sense all along that when psychology was taken fully into account, the monist epistemological view would be the view of the Natural Left and the dualist epistemological view would be the view of the Natural Right. As we saw earlier, the philosophers have never figured it out that way, and neither have the jurisprudential or economic theorists. But the anthropologists apparently have and, as I suggested in an earlier look at Ruth Benedict, part of their monist vision no doubt came from an early commitment to cultural relativity, both as a substantive position and as an anthropological methodology. Even beyond that, however, it seems that the anthropologists had a sense before anyone else that the dialectic comes to a reconciliation and that the separations of method between positivism and antipositivism—particularly as they each became more psychologically pure—ultimately fall under the umbrella of psychologically and cognitively relativistic headings. To put it another way, whereas even in sociology Jan Loubser can call for an abolition of boundaries between method and values, the left-of-center anthropologists, at least for the last half-century, have never permitted such boundaries to exist.[169]

The Best Understanding

Murray Leaf's fine book, *Man, Mind and Science,* is without question the best review of anthropological theory. Though it is not flawless (it reverses Hegel and Kant's epistemology, for example), it has a deep sense of the emerging ideological character of the monist versus dualist argument in epistemology. Further, unlike the epistemological literature of its sister disciplines, where monism and dualism are reversed, anthropology clearly places monistic and dualistic views in their appropriate ideological camps, monism being left and dualism right.[170] The evolution of the Natural Left is not complete in anthropology and, in terms of understanding its major thinkers, the best that even Leaf can do is to confront English positivism with the commentary of Claude Lévi-Strauss that such positivism was "overly descriptive and [had] a classification orientation."[171] But, when speaking of the full integration of the science of understanding as well as of the place of the individual, Leaf properly cites Malinowski and Boas as two figures who represent monism by "rejecting determinism and focusing on the free and purposive individual."[172] Dualism, in contrast, is seen as upholding a clear differentiation between reality and perception, as well as a distinction between form and matter. Both these attributes represent qualities that philosophical dualism once, and too often still, uses to separate the physical and the social sciences. Anthropological monism, in contrast, has rejected the absolutism of deductive principles and relates immediately to appearances and to the perceptions from which they come. There is, in short, an immediate "variability and instability" in human perception; as Leaf puts it, "the *relativity* of individual perspective" is what is important in knowing the world.[173]

Historically, Leaf has some idea, although it is not complete, of the origins of such a relativism. He is correct in finding a good bit of it in the skepticism of Montesquieu, and he sees that true relativism rejects the dualistic rationalism of Descartes. Though Leaf does not see the progress of that evolution as a movement from the logical to the psychological, and though he does not wish to acknowledge the suppleness of a portion of rationalism and the hardness of a segment of skepticism, he is aware that the dualistic tradition favors "certain *factual* understandings of the *mechanism* of human perception."[174] Further, his discussion of the analytic and synthetic traditions, although not specifically psychological, does recognize that the former tends to engage in the relationship of ideas (an internal logic) and that the synthetic perspective deals with matters of fact (importing a fullness of the perception of reality).

Again Leaf is still not fully at the point of relativism in his own criticism of pure logic, particularly as he approves of Kant's method of needing to find a consensus in order to achieve commonalities "in creating ordered affairs."[175] Leaf, unfortunately, classifies Kant as essentially monistic and Hegel as dualistic, perceiving the dialectic as being chronically unresolved and the commonality that Kant searched for as being a unity. Ironically, in discussing Johann Herder, a student of Kant, Leaf acknowledges that Herder's view is more collective and that in its own intellectual milieu, linguistics, it expected "inherent internal variation, variation over space and development over time."[176] These admissions are important and in asserting that man is "no independent substance [but is] connected with all the elements of nature [and] a multitudinous harmony, a living self," Herder argues for what even Leaf acknowledges is a "non-Kantian position," or a position that Leaf says blurs the distinction between the Kantian and Hegelian positions.[177] I would argue that it does not actually blur the distinction and that, within a psychological perspective, the Herder view was epistemologically Hegelian all along.

In any case, the development of late-arriving anthropological theory does mirror the fission-fusion model, although the early roots that would lead back to a logical rationalism and a logical skepticism are perhaps even a little weaker here than they are in sociology. Yet, with the first works of the mid-nineteenth century, psychological directions are becoming quite clear. Both J. J. Bachofen and Adolphe Bastian, in their discussions of primitive religions, for example, searched for internal and even naturalistic structures and either specifically eschewed the search for external sanctions (Bachofen) or wanted psychology, in a truly monistic fashion, to be a part of natural science (Bastian).[178] Though Bastian did not succeed in discovering convincing psychological laws, Leaf points out that these two viewpoints, which are at least faintly rationalistic in a supple way, had a great impact upon Franz Boas and American anthropology generally.

All these views contrasted sharply with those of E. B. Tylor, who attacked Bachofen and Bastian on the question of freedom of will. This position was not altogether psychological, but it was, nonetheless, a left-of-center view in the late nineteenth century. Tylor argued that the freedom-of-will view was unscientific, and it broached a topic that he did not wish to consider: the question of private purpose.[179] Finally, with E. B. Tylor, the influence of Social Darwinism is clear enough, with culture being held to stem only from prior culture, not from the broad skein of history or human invention. The evidence for all cultural study was to come from "its own direct evidence," not from an "obscure pantheism." In Tylor's conservative view, old cultures, as part of evolution, were to be marked for destruction, something that was "urgently needed for the good of mankind."[180] As Marvin Harris states in *The Rise of Anthropological Theory,* Tylor's view represents a "preoccupation with narrow, rather disembodied cognitive issues"[181] and "suffers even more from its neglect of social organization and economics."[182]

The Modern Strain

While psychological nuances only intermittently entered the anthropological positions of the late nineteenth century, the modern dichotomy of dualism and monism reveals its psychological flavor far more openly. Modern dualism and the coalescence of schools that occurred within it during the 1930s exacted predictable epistemological standards, with the logical positivism of some of anthropology predictably reflecting the logical positivism of other social sciences. The Vienna circle, for example, displayed its love for utility and harsh skepticism with such sentiments as those of Otto Neurath, who wanted a "systemization of empirical procedure" much like that of economics's William Jevons.[183] By then, this strain of skeptical thought was clearly out of sympathy with the relativity that skepticism also brought forth, Neurath himself saying that "neither Hegel nor Schelling encouraged a scientific attitude," nor did they propagate "logical analysis or particular theses which would be used directly in the sciences."[184] The Vienna circle, in fact, originally called itself "The Unity of Science Movement" and believed, as Rudolf Carnap said, that science was simply an accumulation of knowledge and therefore the "generalization of science [was] the same as its integration."[185]

Much the same kind of thing happened with the anthropological residue of Durkheim, as thinkers like Lévy-Bruhl dismissed physiology, drew a great division between humans and animals, and sought an identification of internal states, as Leaf noted, "on the basis of social form."[186] The diffusionists held similar views, Leaf admitting that their metaphysical dualism and their insistence on the noninventiveness of cultures was a position that "appears to have neo-Kantian roots."[187] Finally, with the dualists, there was the English A. R. Radcliffe-Brown who, from his rationally empiricist perspective, sought to remove the element of psychology from anthropology entirely and to concentrate solely on the convergence of anthropological elements like rituals and institutions. In toto, the dualists represent a consistent psychological (or, better, antipsychological) position, and it is a position that, by the 1930s, was increasingly distinguishable from a psychological perspective and from the monist view. The monists, though still not in search of a true psychological relativism, were mirroring the new culturally relativistic position at the same time that they became aware of the role that psychology should play within anthropology.[188] Bronislaw Malinowski, a leading monist, held a vision of human existence that organically linked the human actor with the social actor, even though his psychology was still of the stimulus-response variety with its belief in a "plasticity of interests" and its strong endorsement of the widely descriptive behaviorism of Clark L. Hull over the "'atheoretical' materialistic behaviorism of B. F. Skinner."[189] As Adam Kuper points out, Malinowski opposed the diffusionist position that was represented largely by ethnologists, who preferred the classifications of facts radiating from some central point and co-opted the evolutionists, who preferred to study "systems with an internal dynamic in a more sociological setting."[190]

Franz Boas also reflected this early monism, arguing for a recognition of the "just noticeable differences" between peoples under the influence of the psychophysics of Gustav Fechner.[191] Also, Boas searched for the convergence of the soft variables of culture, arguing that only psychological and biological characteristics are worthy of being called law.[192] This position is in considerable contrast with Radcliffe-Brown's call for a " 'scientific' theory that cultural theories could conform to."[193] Interestingly, almost upon his arrival in the United States in 1887, Boas became concerned with the plight of black Americans and fought for black equality until his death in 1942.[194]

Though monism did not prosper in the early part of the century, by the 1930s, the coalescence of rationalism in its more humanistic revivification, along with a kind of skepticism that was similar to Hegel's, was finding itself within the monism of anthropology. The attempts of Ruth Benedict to combat the objectivist notions of many anthropologists are clear in their own psychological dispositions, for she embraced a modern (non-Spencerian-Stimulus-Organism-Response) psychological view by arguing that "a culture, like an individual, is a more or less consistent pattern of thought and action."[195] For Benedict, seeing culture as "more than the sum of [individual] traits" and choosing psychological and subjective interpretations of reality were among her primary anthropological threads.[196] Leaf is correct in suggesting that "there is a hint of some pan-human psychological mechanism" in Benedict's work.[197] Nonetheless, as Margaret Mead points out in one of her works on Benedict, her use of psychology was not an attempt at developing rigid typologies but was a part of an attempt "to demonstrate what an extraordinary range of cultures had existed and might exist."[198]

Yet the early nonrecognition of a deeper unity of Benedict's work with the emerging monist view may have been part of the reason that randomist ideas like Chomsky's were able to hold sway with notions that language, for instance, existed without "sense or meaning."[199] Certainly, Chomsky "is no less solidly oriented to the positivistic tradition"[200] than were others, like Leonard Bloomfield, but Leaf misses the mark when he criticizes Lévi-Strauss's dichotomy between conscious and unconscious thought as Hegelian solipsism.[201] It is those very dichotomies, along with the tension between them and the recognition of both their complementarity and their eventual reconciliation, that are unique to true monism as well as to the position of the Natural Left. Leaf seems to acknowledge the value of such a position when he chastises those who believe that theory is best kept separate from data and conceptual generalities kept separate from concrete particulars, and that the behavior of individuals is solely determined by collectivities. Yet what, I would ask, if there is a subsequent confrontation of these very contradictions? Surely, the Natural Left position of what is still mired in modern dualism looks toward that reconciliation, as Leaf notices himself when he fits "alliance theory" under dualism and finds it to be searching for "some kind of universal substantive symbolism."[202] To be sure, alliance theory is not full relativism, but if even a part of dualism searches for more subtle universals, singular though they may presently be, we stand on the verge of the Natural Left. Surely, the cultural relativism of anthropology that came from a softly rationalistic and relativistic view and that, in turn, was based upon both a personal and a cultural relativity, has moved closer to the Natural Left position than any other social science has.

Writers like Leaf, who search for human essence and a return to description over logic in methodology, are correct in saying that much of the new understanding will grow out of Gestalt psychology. Leaf agrees with the behavioralist Hull that "the human nervous system itself—in the way that Wundt and his successors had described it" is the key to the new ground.[203] Yet rather than trying to find intersubjectivity through language, which I would argue is still an attempt at consensus and not complementarity, Leaf is closer to the mark when he cites Maurice Merleau-Ponty's abhorrence of reductionist and mechanistic psychology and his search for theories that better "accommodate the psychological facts of ambiguity and individual perceptual freedom."[204] Leaf senses that relativity is near, citing Benjamin Lee Whorf's "linguistic relativity" and Victor Turner's relativity of the meaning of symbols in different contexts. Perhaps most favorably, Leaf refers to J. J. Bachofen and Lewis Morgan and their recognition of different kinds of minds as well as to the importance of Eastern, principally Hindu and Buddhist, theory.[205] Though Leaf, again, misidentifies such notions with Kantian rather than Hegelian thought (in great part because he still looks for universals and not for complementarities), he nonetheless perceives that Victor Turner's sense of it all is close to "Bastian's use of Fechner's concept of just-noticeable differences."[206]

How close he is, for, again, the epistemology of the subtle differences lies on the psychological left, *logically* between the two poles of (a) large differences and (b) perfect identity, but psychologically to the left of both of these positions. Leaf ultimately claims that monism is the more robust anthropological model, as surely it is. So too it is the more robust model

THE SOCIAL SCIENCES   *135*

in philosophy and all the other areas that we have looked at, though it has not yet fully emerged from any of them. But if those who search for it within all fields can overcome the notion that what they are looking for is "grounded in a common conception of human nature" and accept both the relativity of human natures and the relativity of epistemologies within the study of humankind, they will soon arrive at the position of the Natural Left.[207] We, for our part, are ready for the investigation of politics.

NOTES

1. Richard Hooker, "The Doctrine of Natural Law," in Robert Lindsay Schuettinger, ed., *The Conservative Tradition in European Thought* (New York: Putnam's, 1970), pp. 128–37.

2. Leonard Krieger, *The Politics of Discretion: Pufendorf and the Acceptance of Natural Law* (Chicago: The University of Chicago Press, 1965), pp. 88 ff.

3. John Locke, "Essays on the Law of Nature," in Paul E. Sigmund, ed., *Natural Law in Political Thought* (Cambridge, Mass.: Winthrop, 1971), pp. 91–95.

4. Quoted in Paul Edwards, ed., *The Encyclopedia of Philosophy* (New York: Macmillan and The Free Press, 1967), vol. 8, p. 264.

5. Daniel Boorstin, *The Mysterious Science of the Law* (Boston: Beacon Press, 1941).

6. Frederick von Savigny, *On the Vocation of Our Age for Legislation and Jurisprudence,* trans. Abraham Hayward (London, 1831), p. 134.

7. Ernest Barker, in Otto Von Gierke, *Natural Law and the Theory of Society* (Cambridge: Cambridge University Press, 1934), p. 1.

8. Roscoe Pound, *Interpretations of Legal History* (Cambridge: Cambridge University Press, 1930), p. 12.

9. Ibid., p. 13.

10. Savigny, *Vocation of Our Age,* p. 135.

11. Ibid.

12. Ibid. (Emphasis mine.)

13. G. F. Puchta, *Outlines of Jurisprudence as the Science of Right—A Juristic Encyclopedia* (Edinburgh, 1887), p. 39.

14. Ibid.

15. Ibid., p. 31.

16. Rudolf Stammler, "Fundamental Tendencies in Modern Jurisprudence," *Michigan Law Review* 21 (1923): 649.

17. Ibid., p. 650.

18. Ibid., p. 865. (Emphasis mine.)

19. Robert Kocourek, *An Introduction to the Science of the Law* (Boston: Little, Brown, 1950), p. 48.
20. Ibid., p. 52.
21. See M. P. Golding, *The Nature of Law* (New York: Random House, 1966), pp. 42–43.
22. Thomas S. K. Scott-Craig, "John Locke and Natural Right," in Arthur L. Harding ed., *Natural Law and Natural Rights* (Dallas: Southern Methodist University Press, 1955), p. 32.
23. Huntington Cairns, *Legal Philosophy from Plato to Hegel* (Baltimore: Johns Hopkins Press, 1949), p. 390.
24. A. P. d'Entreves, *Natural Law* (London: Hutchinson House, 1951), p. 115.
25. Ibid. (Emphasis mine.)
26. A. P. d'Entreves, "Three Conceptions of Natural Law," in M. P. Golding, *Nature of Law*, p. 37.
27. A. P. d'Entreves, *Natural Law*, pp. 70–71.
28. Ibid., p. 99.
29. Ibid., p. 100.
30. Jeremy Bentham, *The Theory of Legislation* (New York: Harcourt, Brace, 1931), p. 82.
31. Ibid.
32. John Austin, *Lectures on Jurisprudence* (London: Campbell, 1869), vol. 2, p. 1107.
33. Ibid.
34. Hans Kelsen, "The Pure Theory of Law," trans. Charles H. Wilson, *Law Quarterly Review* 51 (1935): 517.
35. H. L. A. Hart, "Positivism and the Separation of Law and Morals," *Harvard Law Review* 71 (1958): 596–629.
36. H. L. A. Hart, "Positivism and the Separation of Law and Morals," in R. M. Dworkin, ed., *The Philosophy of Law* (Oxford: Oxford University Press, 1977), p. 17.
37. Ibid., p. 20.
38. Ibid.
39. Ibid.
40. Ibid., p. 26.
41. Ibid., p. 36.
42. Léon Duguit, "Objective Law," *Columbia Law Review* 20 (1920): 829.
43. Roscoe Pound, "A Theory of Social Interests," Papers and Proceedings of the American Sociological Society 15 (1921): 16.
44. Ibid., p. 22.
45. Ibid., p. 29.
46. Ibid., p. 30.
47. Ibid.
48. Dugit, "Objective Law," vol. 21, p. 24.

49. Fuller, *The Law in Quest of Itself* (Boston: Beacon Press, 1940), p. 26.
50. Ibid., p. 47 and p. 77.
51. Golding, *Nature of Law*, p. 167.
52. Ibid., pp. 168–69.
53. Ibid., p. 169.
54. Fuller, *The Law*, p. 121.
55. Ibid., p. 118.
56. Ibid., pp. 118–19.
57. Ibid., p. 114.
58. Ibid.
59. Hart, "Positivism," p. 610.
60. Ibid., p. 565.
61. Ibid., p. 566.
62. Ibid., p. xli.
63. Arthur Harding, "A Reviving Natural Law," in Thomas S. K. Scott-Craig, *Natural Law*, p. 81.
64. Ibid.
65. Ibid.
66. Ibid.
67. Ibid.
68. Ibid.
69. John Rawls, *A Theory of Justice* (Cambridge, Mass.: The Belknap Press, 1971), p. 5.
70. Ibid., p. 12.
71. Ibid.
72. Ibid., p. 253.
73. Ibid.
74. Dworkin, Ronald, "Hard Cases," *Harvard Law Review*, 88 (April 1974–75): 1057.
75. Ibid., p. 1107.
76. Richard Wasserstrom, "Rights, Human Rights and Racial Discrimination," in A. I. Melden, ed., *Human Rights* (Belmont, Calif.: Wadsworth, 1970), pp. 100–101 and 106.
77. Ibid., p. 106.
78. Ibid., p. 401.
79. Robert Denoon Cumming, *Human Nature and History, A Study of the Development of Liberal Thought* (Chicago: The University of Chicago Press, 1969), p. 278.
80. Ibid.
81. Quoted in J. B. Schniewind, *Mill's Essay on Literature and Society* (New York: Collier Books, 1965), p. 263.
82. Ibid.
83. Ibid., p. 120.
84. Cumming, *Human Nature and History*, p. 331.

85. Ibid., p. 384.
86. Eric Roll, *A History of Economic Thought* (London: Faber and Faber, 1956), p. 233.
87. Ibid., p. 212.
88. Ibid., p. 214.
89. Ibid., p. 236.
90. Ibid., p. 306.
91. Ronald L. Meek, "Value in the History of Economic Thought," University of Leicester, England (unpublished paper).
92. John Maynard Keynes, "The General Theory of Employment," *Quarterly Journal of Economics* 51 (February 1937): 209–28.
93. Meek, "Value," p. 4.
94. Roy Harrod, *The Life of John Maynard Keynes* (New York: Harcourt, Brace, 1951), p. 136.
95. Ibid.
96. James L. Cochrane, "Keynesian Probability and the General Theory," *Revisita Internationale di Science e Commerciale* 17 (February 1970): 322.
97. Ibid.
98. Sidney Weintraub, ed., *Modern Economic Thought* (Philadelphia: University of Pennsylvania Press, 1977), pp. 117–18.
99. Thomas Mayer, "David Hume and Monetarism," *Quarterly Journal of Economics* (August 1980): 88–100.
100. Richard McKenzie, "The Neo-Classicists vs. the Austrians: A Partial Reconciliation of Competing World Views," *Southern Economic Journal* 47, no. 1 (July 1980):2.
101. Ibid., p. 5.
102. Ibid., p. 11.
103. Daniel Fusfeld, "The Conceptual Framework of Modern Economics," *Journal of Economic Issues* 14, no. 1 (March 1980): 1.
104. Ibid.
105. Ibid., p. 31.
106. Sherman R. Krupp, "Types of Controversy in Economics," in Sherman R. Krupp, ed., *The Structure of Economic Science* (Englewood Cliffs, N.J.: Prentice-Hall, 1966), pp. 47–48.
107. Jerome Rothenberg, "Values and Value Theory in Economics," in Krupp, ibid., p. 222.
108. G. L. S. Schackle, *Epistemics and Economics* (Cambridge: Cambridge University Press, 1972), p. 5.
109. Lawrence Nabors, "The Positive and Genetic Approaches," in Krupp, *Structure of Economic Science*, p. 68.
110. Leonard Silk, "Economics by Any Other Name," *New York Times*, October 16, 1977, sec. 4, p. 7.
111. James M. Buchanan, "Economics and Its Scientific Neighbors," in Krupp, *Structure of Economic Science*, p. 167.

112. Rothenberg, "Values," p. 227.
113. Fusfeld, "Conceptual Framework," p. 1.
114. Ibid., p. 2.
115. Peter Ekeh, *Social Exchange Theory: The Two Traditions* (London: Heinemann, 1974), p. 13.
116. Conversation with Professor Alice Kosakof, Department of Anthropology, The University of South Carolina.
117. Hans P. M. Andriaansens, *Talcott Parsons and the Conceptual Dilemma* (London: Routledge and Kegan Paul, 1980), p. 9.
118. Anthony Giddens, *Positivism and Sociology* (London: Heinemann, 1974), pp. 24–25.
119. Ibid., p. 31.
120. Werner J. Cahnman, "Max Weber and the Methodological Controversy in the Social Sciences," in Cahnman, Werner, J. ed., *Sociology and History, Theory and Research* (London: The Free Press, 1964), p. 108.
121. Ibid., p. 113.
122. Ibid., p. 116.
123. Paul Edwards, ed., *The Encyclopedia of Philosophy* (New York: Macmillan and The Free Press, 1967), vol. 7, p. 442.
124. Ibid., p. 443.
125. Ibid.
126. Ibid., vol. 2, p. 438.
127. Ibid.
128. Ibid., p. 439.
129. Ralf Dahrendorf, "In Praise of Thrasymachus," in Ralf Dahrendorf, ed., *Essays in the Theory of Society* (Stanford, Calif.: Stanford University Press, 1958), p. 130.
130. Ibid., p. 138.
131. Ibid.
132. Ibid., p. 146.
133. Ibid., p. 149.
134. Ralf Dahrendorf, "Out of Utopia," in Dahrendorf, *Essays*, p. 117.
135. Ibid., p. 121.
136. Ibid., p. 122.
137. Ibid.
138. Adriaansens, *Talcott Parsons*, p. 15.
139. Ibid., p. 16.
140. Ibid., p. 17.
141. Ibid., p. 18.
142. Ibid., p. 25.
143. Ibid., p. 32.
144. Ibid., p. 36.
145. Alvin W. Gouldner, *The Coming Crisis of Western Sociology* (New York: Basic Books, 1970), p. 510.

146. Ibid., p. 511.
147. Ibid., p. 47.
148. Ibid., p. 100.
149. Ibid.
150. Ibid., p. 101.
151. Ibid., p. 103.
152. Ibid., p. 110.
153. Ibid., p. 196.
154. Ibid.
155. Ibid., p. 414.
156. Ibid., p. 497.
157. Richard H. Brown, "The Emergence of Existential Thought: Philosophical Perspectives on Positivist and Humanist Forms of Social Theory," in Jack D. Douglas and John M. Johnson, eds., *Existential Sociology* (Cambridge: Cambridge University Press, 1977), p. 78.
158. Ibid., p. 83.
159. Ibid., p. 84.
160. Ibid., p. 90.
161. Dag Østerberg, *A Meta-Sociological Essay* (Pittsburgh: Duquesne University Press, 1976), p. 12.
162. Ibid., pp. 17–20.
163. Ibid., p. 28.
164. Ibid., p. 34.
165. Ibid., p. 35.
166. Ibid., p. 37.
167. Ibid., p. 39.
168. Ibid., p. 42.
169. Jan J. Loubser, "The Values Problem in Social Science in Developmental Perspective," in Jan J. Loubser et al., eds., *Explanations in General Theory in Social Science* (New York: The Free Press, 1976), p. 82.
170. Murray J. Leaf, *Man, Mind and Science, A History of Anthropology* (New York: Columbia University Press, 1979).
171. Quoted in Leaf, *Man, Mind and Science*, p. 3.
172. Ibid., p. 6.
173. Ibid., p. 7. (Emphasis mine.)
174. Ibid., p. 11. (Emphasis mine.)
175. Ibid., p. 58.
176. Ibid., p. 82.
177. Ibid.
178. Ibid., pp. 118–19.
179. Ibid., pp. 121–22.
180. Ibid., p. 123.
181. Marvin Harris, *The Rise of Anthropological Theory* (New York: Thomas Y. Crowell, 1968), p. 203.

182. Ibid., p. 202.
183. Leaf, *Man, Mind and Science*, p. 153.
184. Quoted in Leaf, *Man, Mind and Science*, p. 153.
185. Ibid., p. 155.
186. Leaf, *Man, Mind and Science*, p. 153.
187. Ibid., p. 164.
188. Ibid., p. 185.
189. Ibid., p. 187.
190. Adam Kuper, *Anthropologists and Anthropology* (New York: Pica Press, 1973), p. 15.
191. Leaf, *Man, Mind and Science*, p. 199.
192. Quoted in Leaf, *Man, Mind and Science*, p. 199.
193. Leaf, *Man, Mind and Science*, p. 200.
194. Marshall Hyatt, *The Emergence of a Discipline* (Ann Arbor, Mich.: University Microfilms, 1980), pp. 187 ff.
195. Leaf, *Man, Mind and Science*, p. 221.
196. Ibid., p. 222.
197. Ibid., p. 223.
198. Margaret Mead, *Ruth Benedict* (New York: Columbia University Press, 1974), p. 44.
199. Leaf, *Man, Mind and Science*, p. 232.
200. Ibid.
201. Ibid., p. 258.
202. Ibid., p. 293.
203. Ibid., p. 300.
204. Ibid., p. 303.
205. Ibid., p. 322.
206. Ibid.
207. Ibid., p. 334.

CHAPTER FOUR

Politics

What, then, does all the foregoing mean for political theory? We began with a reading of Aristotle that asked for a recognition of a subjective step in Aristotle's link to reason. It was a conceptually "horizontal" link, defining a subjectivism that argued for the acceptance of a relativistic human nature and that also suggested that reason itself, as it has been understood in Western thought, is in fact an aggregate concept. It was made up of all the varied images of reason that come from the full range of human perception and value.

We then attempted to identify the origin of that range and suggested that the full spectrum is best understood through the principal ranges of human personality and human cognitive preferences that exist throughout a population. The spatial derivation of the authoritarian model is far from being a complete model of the human psyche, yet it does explain the relative need for a kind of definitional bordering and differentiation in cognitive styles. Further, the model explains these cognitive styles along the same continuum of human psychology that roughly corresponds to the delineation of left-to-right political identifications. By acknowledging the relationship between these two spectra, this psychological model should serve as the most robust of the explanatory devices dealing with the relation of psychology to politics.

What I then suggested was that the psychological variable increasingly bore upon the classical metaethical division between rationalism and skepticism and that it did so particularly as our "knowledge" became more empirical in its nature. The result of this psychological orientation toward the certainty or the alleged certainty of data is that the "rationalists" began to divide themselves between (a) those who embraced that new empiricism and (b) those who attempted to maintain a textural "softness" within the rational position. At the same time, the skeptical position divided itself between (a) those who preferred to believe that the world contained no order whatsoever and (b) those who were skeptical primarily of exaggerated claims for certainty concerning that order. As we have said, the psychological distinction within the two classical positions eventually superseded the logical distinctions between the two. New coalitions were formed, and the rationalists who had rejected the intellectual purities that preceded the French Revolution created an alliance with the relativists among the former skeptics. The more empirically demanding of the rationalists felt increasingly more comfortable with groups like the nihilistic neo-Kantians and the utilitarians.

Again, at least by the end of the nineteenth century, the fundamental process of metaethical realignment was largely complete. Similar realignments were also beginning to emerge within the disciplines of economics, law, and so forth. In all these fields, the broad similarity of what occurred and the general coincidence of time during which it occurred are indicators of the increasing influence of the psychological variable and the metaethical realignment. But beyond these more obvious benchmarks, the new coalescences within the metaethical schools, as well as the coalescence of positions within the various subfields, illustrated the difficulty that the left was having at one end of the continuum.

As a result, the right won an early acceptance as the intellectually orthodox view—and whether we accentuate the often gross misunderstandings of the work of Hegel (with the resultant diminution of what should have been a vast intellectual influence on the left), or whether we reflect upon the inability of formal social science to counterpoise broader balances within its all-too-practical equilibriums—the left seems to have nearly always come up short. Clearly, all this had a substantial impact upon political theory as well.

Within the arenas of political theory and real-world politics, nineteenth- and twentieth-century orthodoxy imposed the same logical and orthodoxy-reinforcing prejudices that we have seen elsewhere. Political theory carried the burden of serving both as a distiller of the thinking that flowed from other disciplines and as a unique refining agent between its own theories and the realities of contemporary politics. To a degree, of course, law, economics, and all disciplines reflect their intellectual neighbors as well as human reality. But politics as a discipline is even more severely stretched both by its neighboring disciplines and by the real world. At one level, it carries the burden of ideology for all of social science, and its resultant, peculiarly hybrid nature may be part of what has accounted for a delay in the emergence of the Natural Left within both its own theory and the actuality of politics. In an ironic sense, the study of political theory, because of its ideological burdens as well as because of its closeness to the most immediate of public realities, is handicapped more severely than any other intellectual discipline in its search for stable foundations.

History, particularly the modern history of real politics, has unfortunately contributed greatly to this intellectual ambiguity. What has often been included under the definitions of the Left within, say, the last three hundred years, could hardly be more diverse. The overthrow of the Stuarts in 1688 and the 1968 student march to the Renault works were so different in their goals and in the psychological dispositions of their participants that it strains all sense of definition to place them within a single ideological category at one end of the political spectrum. Indeed, the many chasms that lie between varied political events illustrate the magnitude of the obstacles to finding the Natural Left position in politics. Certainly, a part of what makes up the Left includes the freeing of new sets of peoples to become politically active. It also allows these peoples to rebel over newer and perhaps more subtle grievances.

The conventional depictions of the Left that typified the early stages of modern radicalism are largely representational. They were concerned primarily with the inclusion of a previously disfranchised populace into evolving democratic political systems. These same depictions have usually found more modern stages of the Left to be concerned with economic distributions. Nonetheless, even this depiction ignores the greater difficulties that the Left has had in comparison to the Right in the development of its position. A rough sense of egalitarianism was rarely a match for the well-established and more understandable notion of a strictly hierarchical view of the political order. The linkage of a psychological predilection for a well-ordered social system with the traditional conservative socialization of most nation-states no doubt enhanced the possibility for an earlier coalescence of one side of the realignment's emerging politics.

Even more significant in the delaying of the Natural Left position was that in its early period, the political Left frequently was dominated by those whose personality was anything but that of the true or Natural Left. Whether it was the Benthamite "Radicals" of the English nineteenth century or the middle-class burghers of Germany in 1848, the Robespierres of the French Revolution or the Lenins of the Russian Revolution, the vanguard of the Left was in so many cases dominated by those who were, if anything, quite conservative psychologically. As we review the theoretical underpinnings and, in some cases, the actual behavior of movements that purported to be radical in their orientation, let us observe how many of these "Left" movements neither had their roots in, nor in turn contributed anything to, the theoretical position of a Natural Left.

The American Example

The illusions that for so long delayed leftward theoretical evolution were probably nowhere more apparent than in the United States. The entreaties of figures like Thomas Paine and Thomas Jefferson, and the creation of what was a genuinely democratic experiment, very quickly became the principal testing ground for a resurgence of the psychological and political Right. The theoretical foundation for such a retrenchment is clear within the writings of the fathers of the Constitution, and particularly within James Madison's Federalist No. 10. This work is not only a monument to the defeat of the aspirations of what remained of the American Left of its day; it stands as well as a still influential rationalization for an absence of the very investigations that would have accommodated the Natural Left. As Madison was determined to build a structure within the federal government that would absorb a popular, collective will and diffuse it, the nineteenth-century writings of the South Carolinian John C. Calhoun also obstructed collectivism through its insistence upon nullification and the concurrent majority. Though the American Confederacy, of which Calhoun was the intellectual godfather, failed in its secession attempt, the direction of postwar arrangements (the settlement of the disputed 1876 presidential election and the judicial abandonment of the Civil War Amendments in particular) indirectly reinforced the theoretical notions of both economic individualism and philosophical atomism.

One additional American theorist should be mentioned in this context. The writings of William James, a late-nineteenth-century figure who elevated pragmatism to a kind of intellectual respectability, could have achieved prominence only within a nation that already held to its deeply antitheoretical bias. James's thoughts on pragmatism are a marvel of revulsion at the theoretical process itself. They not only contain a dogged justification of freedom from grand theory but also portray the psychological predispositions of James within that peculiarly Americanized hybrid of Lockean Natural Right, Spencerian Social Darwinism, and the native Madisonian ideal of collective impotence.

The seemingly mellow openings to *Pragmatism,* including such disclaimers of bias as James's plea for not viewing the dichotomous "passions" of the mind as rivals, soon give way to a series of harsh rebukes to what James calls "the rationalistic temper."[1] From a friendly concession that "more universality or extensiveness is . . . one mark which the philosopher's conceptions must possess," as well as from an acknowledgment that that kind of extensive mind needs to have the "causes [of events] converge to a minimum number," James turns on the rationalist whom he claims "accuses us [the pragmatists] of denying truth" while he (the rationalist) "substitutes a pallid outline for the real world's richness." In the place of a balance between what James well understood of two types of minds, he climaxes his assault by claiming that "[s]urely in this field of truth it is the pragmatists and not the rationalists who are the more genuine defenders of the universe's rationality."[2]

Thus, the biases of James and the biases that have typified much of American political thought would hardly have furthered the recognition, much less the coalescence, of a Natural Left. Indeed, James, in his own failure to recognize the biases of pure logic, argues that "the conditional ways in which we do think are so much irrelevance and matter for psychology. Down with psychology, up with logic."[3] The last disclaimer speaks for itself. The Natural Left could only be stillborn with that level of nourishment, and indeed, what little of a Natural Left exists within the United States is usually found outside the arenas of politics. The satiric prose of Mark Twain and the lyric poetry of Walt Whitman are still the finest examples of true American radicalism.

Thus, the American experience, within what originally may have been at least a mildly "revolutionary" political climate, evidences only a precipitous retreat from any leftward direction. America, indeed, is an extraordinary example of how an indigenous *psychological* right (or a logical left) can lock itself into what passes for a radical political position and then emerge in a position of leadership as the orthodox left gains credibility and support. The American experience also illustrates how difficult it is for the Natural Left to emerge out of a realpolitik that is so heavily imbued with an antitheoretical bias. The contributions of a theorist like Victor Berger are rare in the American experience, and even Berger's theoretical bent was overshadowed by his penchant for tight political organization within a psychologically conservative German-American city like Milwaukee, Wisconsin.[4] His style conflicted with that of Eugene Debs, whom he brought to socialism but who was uncomfortable with organization and like his successor in socialism, Norman Thomas, Debs may have represented a Natural Left better than the theorists.[5] Nonetheless, the antitheoretical bent of both Debs and Thomas insured that their radicalism never developed within a highly individualistic culture like that of the United States. The nascent psychology of these views remained stillborn. Indeed, even the so-called New Left of the 1960s, with Tom Hayden's notions of "consciousness" of "our own subjective concerns," represented only vaguely psychological themes.[6] The arguments for atomized "participatory" solutions undermined any theoretical foundation for the Natural Left.

The European Experience

The European experience, particularly that of the Continent, of course, is one that has been far more theoretical than that of America. The English Left, as well as never being highly theoretical, was rather consistently inhibited by what one writer called the "intricate complex of social inhibitions, safety valves, recreational outlets, economic relationships, snobberies and periods of enlightened government which made of the British worker a reformist."[7]

Clearly, such a complex of civilizing forces was responsible for much of England's avoidance of serious social and political upheaval after the Industrial Revolution. But, just as clearly, the predominance of utopian over socialist and particularly confrontational socialist positions within England also accounted for the relative peacefulness of nineteenth-century British politics. Robert Owen and William Godwin, the early utopians, were precursors of the Natural Left, with a harmonious view of the world and an optimistic view of human nature both being prominent in their writings. We have already discussed how British radicalism, so called, soon lapsed into a utilitarianism that was clearly of the psychological right. But Mill's largely frustrating struggle to get out from under utility at least reflected the spirit of humanism that was soon revivified by the Fabians. To be sure, the Fabians were not purely of the Natural Left any more than were all utopians, one writer suggesting that there was "perhaps too much of the social-scientist looking at human beings and their doings as something to be organized, arranged, put right."[8]

Certainly, the Fabians were hardly conscious of their psychological predispositions, and they usually put "their advocacy of socialism on a basis, not of emotion, but of reason and information." They thus often concluded with recommendations for the deep involvement of the state in the nation's economic life.[9] Nonetheless, the English strains of left-of-center thought did reflect a gentler, more humanistic view, and into the present time that approach to the Natural Left seems to have continued. R. H. Tawney certainly sought to "work out a new social synthesis," as he called it, in order to "provide more compelling motives for the sustained co-operative effort which . . . civilization demands."[10] His early-twentieth-century writings consciously tried to appeal, "not only to the interests, but to the conscience and reason, of all men of good will" as they embraced the influences of literature, art, education and religion, "as well as [those] in the dusty world of politics."[11]

To a considerable degree, that ideal remains, even with the recent Labour party trending away from Harold Wilson's vision of a nonconfrontational and "uniquely relevant"[12] philosophy based upon the spirit of the trade association, the cooperative societies, and church and chapel. These needs are presently met, perhaps, with the creation of a new Social

Democratic party that better represents class harmony and even transnational integration than does the original party of the Fabians. To be sure, the English, unlike their continental neighbors, were blessed with governmental and legal institutions that permitted a higher degree of civility to accompany the dramatic social changes of the first industrialization and beyond. Yet, still, the balance between the logical left and the psychological left in the United Kingdom speaks rather well for a nation that, though considered to be individualistic and competitive in many theoretical overviews, has perhaps come further than any other nation had toward the evolution of a Natural Left.

The continent of Europe, of course, has been a place of considerably more ferment in both political theory and activity than has either England or the United States. In many ways, the strains of radicalism were richer and more varied there, but it must also be said that so much of what passed for radicalism turned out to either fall back into liberalism and technical reforms or into the more severe forms of confrontational socialism. Overall, I would suggest that the left-of-center theorists of Europe, for reasons that were only in part related to political institutions, were more prone to fall into traditional, economic kinds of confrontations and lose the spirit of even their own utopian idealists. The heritage of people like Charles Fourier was largely lost in such an atmosphere, and Fourier's incredibly psychological early-nineteenth-century writings that spoke of instinctual repression and the existence of human desires and appetites were soon ignored by the emerging orthodoxy of socialism.[13] It has taken a long time indeed to return to a substantial Left position that included a consideration of rotating work schedules, differences in tastes and temperments, and feminist questions; and the relative disregard of such issues by so many socialists was surely part of the reason that Fourier's issues unsuccessfully sought prominence for so long.

The early work of Henri de Saint-Simon reveals one line of retreat from continental utopianism, with the Frenchman's faith in technocracy and *les industriels* revealing a deep commitment (along with his successful real estate ventures during the French Revolution) to the economic enterprise. Though often called a socialist, Saint-Simon courted the entrepreneurs throughout his career, and despite the large following that did collect around him, his major contributions are still sometimes remembered as those relating to the improvement of the French banking system and to improved canalization within France.[14]

Within a few years after the death of Saint-Simon, the French Left was deeply divided between two figures with recognizable psychological differences. Louis Blanqui called for violent revolution if the need arose and foresaw such revolution as being generated by secret elitist societies that would terrorize the bourgeoisie. His early form of anarcho-syndicalism drew deep class-related lines, and he called for a group of professional revolutionaries to take on the entrepreneurs in the service of, rather than in cooperation with, the proletariat itself.[15]

Louis Blanc, by contrast, was essentially a reformer, a democrat, and one who believed in an "associationist" view of the workplace, thus avoiding the authoritarianism of either private- or state-owned capital and proprietorship.[16] Blanc is thought by some to be a forerunner of the English Fabians, and his distaste for deep class divisions and militant confrontation was evidenced, among other things, by his refusal of support for the Paris Commune. Unfortunately, at that time the influence of the more logically left radical position was more substantial than was the influence of the more psychologically left position. Indeed, even the anarchism of someone like Pierre Proudhon only furthered the psychologically conservative position. Ironically, of all the figures we have looked at or will look at, perhaps none drew deeper and finer lines than did this Frenchman who believed in inherent inequalities among the races and in the inferiority of women, and who was anglophobic and anti-Semitic as well as antiproperty.[17]

Again, the clear pattern of French left-wing thought and the events of 1848 and 1871 demonstrate an imbalance in favor of the logical over the psychological left. The stage was set for the influence of Marxism (which will be discussed separately) and the decline of utopianism, much as it was for the Germans at the same time. Briefly, the German experience saw the eclipse of Hegelian epistemological idealism and those early pre-Marxian communist notions that held to a serene and harmonious human condition. Wilhelm Witling's League of the Just, for example, was opposed by so many who, like Karl Schapper, insisted upon the anti-utopian view, and the class-transcending thought of Moses Hess and his democratically inclined student, Ferdinand Lassalle, also fell prey to the tenets of Marxian materialism and class antagonism.[18] Though the revisionist position of post-Marxian thinkers like Eduard Bernstein retreated from much of the antidemocratic confrontationalism of Marx and Engels, its own credibility demanded that its appeals be largely economic and not psychological.

Certainly, the reasons for an economic emphasis may in part have been a result of institutional concerns such as the lateness of Germany's national reconciliation. Yet, without question, the triumph of socialism on the Continent only postponed the evolutionary emergence of the Natural Left. Many of these socialist movements proved to be extraordinarily right wing, the fascism of both Italy and Germany being the extreme examples, of course. Among the more moderate of the continental socialist movements, and even within the United Kingdom, there has been a tendency toward slippage to the right under socialist doctrine and governance. The causes of this slippage are manifold, but a willingness to accept less of an economic redistribution than was originally thought just, and more important, a willingness to accept a brittle routinization of bureaucracy within the organization of work as well has typified much of modern socialism. Some of the compromise in everyday politics may always be attributed to the impact of Ramsay MacDonald-like opportunism, but the phenomenon is, again, much a part of the logical versus psychological distinction. Few have understood these phenomena until lately, but what emerges prominently in the New Left European movements of the late 1960s and 1970s does carry the position of the Natural Left forward for the first time in a good while.

One of the writers who is aware of the pitfalls of pure socialism, and particularly Marxian socialism, is the Frenchman Richard Gombin, who in *Les Origins du Gauchisme* traces the modern Left, finds psychological themes throughout much of it, and also sees modern continental radicalism as still in a very developmental period.[19] He suggests that the modern Left has already been largely successful in restoring the original Hegelian and dialectical directions to the Left. Yet Gombin is selective in his approval of the still diverse modern left-of-center European movements, though he clearly favors the early denunciations of orthodox communism that are found in the writings of Raymond Aron, Albert Camus, Maurice Merleau-Ponty, and even the early Jean-Paul Sartre.[20]

These writers clearly reveal their humanistic disapproval of the increasingly bureaucratic nature of state communism, and, more positively, Gombin cites a number of more theoretically inclined writers who sought understandings that addressed the rigidities of Marxism. Included in this group are Karl Korsch, Anton Pannekoeck, Max Horkheimer, and of course the Frankfurt school's father of *The Authoritarian Personality*, T. W. Adorno.[21] Without question, the direction of Gombin's work, along with his criticism and praise of others, is psychologically left. Yet, for all its insight, even Gombin's work does not embrace or create a full psychological theory of politics. What is more, there is little of psychological relativism in any of his own work or in his praise for compatible efforts. To be sure, Gombin consciously repudiates fixed ideologies and argues instead for a recognition of the spontaneities and autonomies of new forms in the world's passing to its next historical stage. His rejection of the bureaucratic state mirrors this antitheoretical bias, particularly as it lauds Merleau-Ponty's *Les Aventures de la Dialectique*, the first major critique of the Bolshevik state. Further, Gombin's embracing of the early German school (largely Hegelian) generally demonstrates his approval of the critical, logically skeptical method of the early rather than the late Marx. Finally, Gombin is intrigued by Korsch's and Lukac's attempts to reestablish revolutionary theory on a dialectical basis, and he heartily approves of Pannekoek's criticism of Lenin's regression to bourgeois materialism.[22]

In short, though Gombin is hardly at the point of a full psychological theory of politics, much less at a theory based upon psychological relativity, the repudiation of the class-dominated and economically deterministic notions of Marx, along with the encouragement of all strata to cure the "banalization" of their everyday lives, reveals, at the least, a deep consciousness of the importance of the psychological condition. In this sense, Gombin is much influenced by the situationist heirs to the lettrist movement. He is also impressed by the situationists' ideal of a psychologically fulfilling artistic and culturally rewarding life for all citizens.

The Last Impediment

With Gombin as perhaps the best representative of the European Left of recent years, there has thus been a clear movement away from economic concerns and an equally clear movement toward psychological questions. As it has attempted to return to a political tradition that was rich with the Hegelian tradition, including its dialectic and its quest for organic harmony in political theory, this newer version of the left has looked to psychology to fill the obvious voids. What I suggest, of course, is that this is now the time for a full psychological theory of politics and that this new theory of politics would do well to begin with the notion of psychological relativity. Why has this not been done sooner? Why has the concept of human *natures* taken so long to assume its rightful place at the core of political theory? The reason, I suggest, is rather clear; and it is that there has been an overweaning influence on the left of one person who for so long has insured that no progress could be made. The individual, of course, is Karl Marx, and it is now time to look at him more closely. If we do not deal with the legacy of Marx quite firmly, the Natural Left will remain unborn for a long time to come.

Although Marx did not much believe in the existence of an inherent nature within man, he at least perceived man's nature as being the sum or the totality of his social relations, and this position is substantially a humanistic view. Yet, though there is some awareness of the differences among various contributions, and though Marx discusses this thoroughly in works like the *Critique of the Gotha Programme,* Marx nevertheless adheres to a predominantly "vertical" or economic valuation standard of "unequal endowment and thus productive capacity" as his chief paradigm. Further, when speaking of the reward side of the contributory model, Marx seems to recognize that there will be an unequal drawing from "the social consumption fund," as he called it, largely because of such things as that "one worker is married; another not; one has more children than another, and so on and so forth."[23] Thus, even in Marx's attempts to deal most directly with contribution and reward in what might be a vaguely relativistic way, his criticisms of inequalities within current contribution-and-reward structures still do not transcend an examination of only differentiated *economic* contributions.

Among Marx's writings, *The Economic and Philosophical Manuscripts* are still cited as evidence for Marx's "humanist" position, and clearly the extension of the concept of alienation beyond the English notion of property transference does reflect a psychological sense within Marx. Also, the references to alienation from a work product or from a fellow worker, as well as the use of a form of the classical negation that seeks to reveal the contradictions of capitalism, indicate a kind of integrated style of reason, perhaps best placed within the Mitroff dichotomy as being the work of the divergent mind.

And yet, I would still contend that the appearance of a humanist notion, or the use of a vaguely psychological reference, is a few steps away from the creation of a psychological theory and there is no question that the predominant difficulty with current Marxism, both in its theory and in its practice, is that an inordinate emphasis is still placed upon the existential and external conditions of the society. At its worst, this emphasis has resulted in what has been called a modern "commodity fetishism," a view of economics that is too concerned with the "technical relations" of production and too isolated from any social framework. At its best, it is a call for little more than a restructuring of the economic relationships of a society in a more "humanistic" way, those production-oriented relationships still being viewed as the principal foundations of any polity.

Marx himself, perhaps, may have had some sense of the assimilation of economic and social or even psychological considerations; but, as we know, the character of the considerations that he included was largely built upon the significance of economic classes. Such a construct is clearly a vertical as well as an "objective" genre of dialectical opposition; references to the human condition aside, there is clearly no prescription within Marx for a psychological or even a more consciously subjective view. This omission is nowhere more apparent than in Marx's discussion of value, a subject to which he devoted a great deal of attention and one that, I believe, is peculiarly adaptable to a set of broader psychological concerns. It is here that Marx argued for why labor value should be considered as more than a matter of economic exchange, that is, why value should be more than a comparison of the magnitude of labor contributed and measured within an economic market. In his quest for a reduction of the importance of the exchange market as a determinant of that value, Marx promised a more abstract view of labor, wishing it to be valued before it came into a place that was contaminated with the capital of the industrialists. But even this concept of labor in the abstract, Marx warned, must be used cautiously, for if the abstract concept meant only a kind of generalization of labor once it was in the market, then the cutting of the valuation of the labor could be sustained over the Marxian insistence on the inherent value of labor itself.

In one sense, Marx's insistence on evaluating labor before it reached the market was much like Ricardo's argument for labor *embodied* over Malthus's notion of labor *commanded,* and in that sense it may still be a radical notion. But, at the same time, this emphasis upon labor value in an economic sense has permitted an ostensibly radical evaluation within Marx to sustain a severe slippage into the calculus of formal economics. I would argue that Marx's materialistic epistemology has in fact impeded the very process of *psychological* abstractness, or what might be a broadly rationalistic determination of the worth of someone's contribution. I would argue further that the materialistic epistemology that underlies Marxism—that is, the rejection of Hegel's notion of the primacy of the mind or the Idea—has doomed Marxist economics and philosophy to an acceptance of a usage of the term "abstractness" that explains only false economic valuation in a market.

Marx's unwillingness to use Hegel's Idealism, and ultimately, Marx's unwillingness to deal with a subjective or even a nascent psychological relativism, have forestalled intellectual movement beyond an analysis of economic value. For the latter omission, for the noninclusion of a systematic understanding of human value over and above economic value, we can be mildly forgiving of Marx. The understanding of human psychology was not then what it is now. But the conscious rejection of Hegel's Idealism, along with the rejection of the embryonic relativism that such an epistemological bias intends, is far more serious in its impact.

In reverting to the epistemology of Ludwig Feuerbach and materialism, Marx failed to see that even such a radical substantive argument that one worker might be equal to another obscures the possibility of one citizen's contribution being qualitatively different from another's, and therefore more difficult to calculate than when the genre of each contribution is similar. Again, Marx obstructed further intellectual progression on the left, for even in his more broad-ranging and diligent condemnation of the exchange market's distortion of true value, he found it necessary to restrict the investigation of the market's distortion to little more than a matter of economic valuation.

As an alternative, a continuation of the Hegelian epistemology would more likely have moved the abstraction of human valuation into a relativist and aggregative setting. It is within such a conceptualization that both the differentiation of psychological being itself and the questions surrounding relative human valuation in view of that differentiation are understood. With epistemological materialism, the place for the suspended dialectic, and for the consideration of the significance of static human complementarity is foreclosed. It is no wonder that Marx's stages of a revised Hegalian dialectic were all economic. Surely Hegel, were he here to comment on it, would not have taken Marx's qualitatively similar stages seriously at all, but then for Marx, the end of the reflexiveness of Montesquieu and of the primacy of the Idea as it came from Hegel could have done nothing else than foreclose the possibility of discovering the next construct. As a consequence, it foreclosed the finding of the next political Left.

Thus, I say again that it is Marx, more than anyone else, who has prevented an earlier understanding of the Natural Left, a circumstance that squares so well, incidentally, with the notion that the psychological proclivity for the externals of epistemological materialism is exactly what the triumph of materialism over Idealism represented psychologically. It is really very much the same kind of phenomenon, of course, as Kierkegaard's triumph of existentialism over essence. Existentialism, like Marxism, was avant garde within the context of the nineteenth century because the principal metaethical axis had not turned sufficiently in its rotation and because the disparity of objective "verticals" was often of such a magnitude that an immediate substantive concern dominated the latent epistemological biases. Nonetheless, the transition to materialism or existentialism—or the trade-off of the short run for the long run within the Left politically or ethically—was very plausible to the Left at that time; and, again, it was this very compromise that made it so difficult for the Natural Left to free itself from Marxist influence.

In concluding this chapter, may I suggest that if knowledge as knowledge still possesses its natural hierarchy that is, if the biases of epistemology still affect method and if the biases of method still transcend the substance of metaphysics or any discipline—then it should be clear that the biases that underlie the metaethical groupings of knowledge themselves must surely have tremendous impact upon substantive theory within the various disciplines. If this is true, then has not an examination of to what degree that metaethical configuration has become influenced by the ranges within human psychology been long overdue in coming? Can we not now, through a novel understanding of the division among the metaethical schools, come upon both an understanding of the balances within the aggregate of human nature and the balances within our intellectual disciplines and our realpolitik, which, after all, are what make up Aristotle's subjective precondition for reason?

Is it so surprising, really, that even among the most recent of the allegedly radical positions many current Marxists wish now to rekindle the early and protopsychological strain of humanism within the writings of Marx? The instincts of Herbert Marcuse or Erich Fromm should not be unexpected. When Fromm, for example, says that "many Marxist Socialists . . . have become aware of the fact that Marxist theory is in need of a psychological theory,"[24] I would certainly agree. Of course Marxism is in need of a psychological theory, but why bother? Even Fromm, a prominent Marxist psychologist, never ventured to build a psychological theory upon the relativity of man's nature. Even he, who called for the inclusion of psychology within Marxist theory, was so divorced from the epistemological and ultimately psychological roots of the left that he could not see the relativity of human nature or the potential relativity of either political theory or the theories of other disciplines. For Fromm, as for so many others, it was almost as if Hegel no longer existed after the appearance of Marx.

Perhaps they could simply not bring themselves to realize that Hegel was doing just fine without Marx and that he was doing find standing on his feet before Marx attempted to turn him upside down. I certainly think that he was and I would argue that Hegel, in fact, is so clearly to the left of Marx that little serious political theory—particularly after the current degree of the metaethical rotation has taken place—can now be considered without the inclusion of the psychological Hegel. If neither liberal democracies nor social democracies nor Marxist nations have discovered the Natural Left in their politics, and if no formerly or presently "progressive" ideologies have spawned the Natural Left in their writings, I would suggest that we have nowhere to go but back to the epistemological fundamentals and begin to build a wholly new theory.

We are now ready for a psychological theory of politics, one that is based, not on human nature, but on the relative human natures that live within the human population. The metaethical axis has nearly completed its quarter turn, and the current discordancy of even the most progressive of political writings is only one of the signs that a Hegelian epistemology and the primacy of the psychological range are now ready to come center stage.

NOTES

1. William James, in Albuirey Castell, ed., *Essays in Pragmatism* (New York: Hafner, 1952), p. 154.
2. Ibid.
3. Ibid., p. 152.
4. Sally M. Milles, *Victor Berger and the Promise of Constructive Socialism* (Westport, Conn.: Greenwood Press, 1973), pp. 38–40.
5. Murray B. Seidler, *Norman Thomas: Respectable Rebel* (Syracuse, N.Y.: Syracuse University Press, 1961), p. 275.
6. Tom Hayden, "The Port Huron Statement," in Teodori Massimo, ed., *The New Left* (Indianapolis: Bobbs-Merrill, 1969), p. 164.
7. David Caute, *The European Left* (New York: McGraw-Hill, 1966), p. 84.
8. T. L. Jarman, *Socialism in Britain* (London: Victor Gollancz, 1972), p. 94.
9. Ibid.
10. R. H. Tawney, *The Radical Tradition* (New York: Pantheon Books, 1964), p. 140.
11. Ibid.
12. Harold Wilson, *The Relevance of British Socialism* (London: Wiedenfeld and Nicolson, 1964), p. 1.
13. George Lichtheim, *The Origins of Socialism* (New York: Praeger, 1969), p. 31.
14. Ibid., pp. 40, 44, 45.
15. Ibid., p. 63.
16. Ibid., pp. 78–79.
17. Ibid., p. 86.
18. Ibid., p. 167.
19. Richard Gombin, *Les Origins du Gauchisme* (Paris: Editions du Seuil, 1971).
20. Ibid., pp. 37–85.
21. Ibid., pp. 63–71.
22. Ibid., p. 71.
23. Karl Marx, "Critique of the Gotha Programme," in Robert C. Tucker, ed., *The Marx-Engles Reader,* 2d ed. (New York: W. W. Norton, 1978), pp. 530–37.
24. Erich Fromm, *Socialist Humanism* (Garden City, N.Y.: Anchor Books, 1966), p. 230.

CHAPTER FIVE

An Emerging Philosophy of Politics

And so, the theory. Let us look first at a simple exchange. If two persons bargain over the value of a commodity or over the labor that produced that commodity, and if the psychologies of these two persons are different, then as long as only the dynamics of the economic bargain or the exchange itself are considered, there will be a predictable inequity in the transaction. The logical left has never addressed more than one kind of inequity. It is the economic inequity, one that has typically resulted from the economic domination of labor in the valuation of its work. Of course, economic domination causes economic inequity, but the extraction of surplus value is a single form of dominance, and it is only one of three forms. There is also an economic inequity that is the result of the interaction of different psychologies, and finally, there is a psychological inequity that results from the interaction of different psychologies.

Of the latter two inequities, the first, having to do with an economic imbalance caused by psychological interaction, is the result of the differentiated personal valuation of both the purchased item and the medium of exchange. The conservative personality values both of these elements differently from the left personality, and these differentiations are important to the valuational and bargaining procedure that occurs between the two bargaining personalities. If, for example, a seller and a buyer are not of a similar disposition toward external commodity valuations, then the two parties to that transaction will value the commodity, the labor, or the exchange at a greater or a lesser value than will the other party. At first, this differentiation may seem of little concern, for each personality appears to value the commodity or the labor bargained for, along with its medium of exchange, in roughly equal proportion. In other words, it might appear that the effect of the differentiated personalities falls evenly upon both sides of the economic transaction. But this is not what happens. The "evening out" occurs only at the time of the original estimation of value by the two parties, and such valuation does not include the subsequent interactions that occur in negotiating and bargaining throughout the production-to-consumption chain. It is here, within the multiple steps of bargaining that are a part of modern trade, that the effect of personality transcends economics.

We know that the conservative personality identifies with "external" qualities. It prefers both the good and the exchange more strongly than does the left personality, and it does so out of a natural preference for those things which are external and more clearly defined. The external nature of both the commodity and the exchange is what makes that saliency higher for the lines personality; thus, when the bargaining that ostensibly is directed toward the compromise between the separate valuations of the parties begins, the lines personality's deeper identification with both elements of the transaction renders the valuational process deeply biased. Again, this imbalance has nothing to do with the economic imbalances that have preoccupied the logical left. It is a description of a purely psychological leverage that creates its own economic imbalance.

This second imbalance parallels a third and even more profound inequity, one that exacts a psychological cost as a result of a psychological imbalance. Economic transactions, particularly modern transactions, are of an almost purely exchange nature. Increasingly, they are denuded of their social character, being less a part of a social form or order than was true within traditional societies. The logical left may have had some sense of this absence within contemporary societies, but there is no sense within the writings of the logical left of either the psychological origins of that loss or of the consistent placement of its burden upon only the left personality.

Yet if we return to the basic Aristotelian notion, that is, to the question of contribution to a polity, we can begin to make out the outlines of the "horizontal" contribution notion. That is, if we have a sense of the idea that the contribution of the left personality is qualitatively different from that of the right, then the analysis of how the left personality is denied its appropriate return can work its way through both the psychological causes of interpersonal economic dominance and the psychological causes of an unbalanced psychological reward. Again, the core of the analysis lies within the psychological disposition of the conservative personality. The lines personality will insist that society's valuations ensure the economic character of the modern transaction, as for that personality a bargain is a bargain, edges to edges. In short, it is the very trading of the commodity for a moneyed value, or the comparing of some precise and universally valued commodity for a similar kind of value, that is favorable to the conservative mind. With the politically significant question of economic valuation as well as the mechanistic determination of such value as it is in turn based upon the formal notions of cost, demand, supply, and things of that nature, modern society yields to its conservative psychological preference. The exclusion of other forms of valuation within the society assures the exclusion of noneconomic interpersonal valuations from each economic transaction, and as the biases within the modern transaction are thus negotiated between atomized, homogeneous entities, they result in psychological imbalances within the community.

What, specifically, are those imbalances, and why do they not fall more evenly? As we have said, it is partly a matter of the relatively higher identification of the conservative personality with the externality of the economic idiom. Yet there is more to the relativity of psychology than a differentiated identification with externals. There is also a deep psychological preference for a cognitive activity here, a preference for the acceptance and reinforcement of a particular way of thinking and working. If there are differences within the human population over the preferences of how people think, then what is most significant for political ideology, as well as for the study of individual preference, is that the effect of these cognitive preferences will manifest itself within the psychological equilibriums of a polity.

Remember that we began with an individual transaction, and I suggested that three biases existed within the modern exchange. Along with these biases, however, there is the simple fact that the personality that is favored within transactions prefers to continue the framework of such dealings. It is that preference, as it is expressed within the larger political arena, that continues to support the imbalance of economic versus noneconomic considerations in public affairs; and it is that preference that would deny a reincorporation of traditional, more balanced psychological castings around individual transactions. In short, this bias forestalls deeper consideration of the noneconomic variables within a polity.

Curiously, what most twentieth-century economists, along with their "policy" counterparts in various social science fields, have invented to redress their perception of imbalance has been a consideration of notions like "externalities" and "public goods." But the inclusion of easily defined considerations like pollution, noise, and the misuse of resources within rigid formulas can never redress the deep epistemological biases of the economic model. If there is to be a political position that is definitive for the Natural Left, it must begin with a redefinition of the very notion of productivity, and such a definition will approach psychological balance only by restoring the appropriate equities among all of society's contributions and rewards.

Let it be clear again that a psychological model of contribution is consistent with the contribution model that Aristotle created in the *Politics*. For Aristotle, the weighing of contribution was never purely vertical or economic. He included horizontal considerations, that is, those things which we now recognize as being largely psychological in nature, and he recognized the need for a wide range of contributions with respect to any society's well-being. Perhaps both Adam Smith and Karl Marx had some sense of the issues of the routinization of work and the alienation of a worker. Yet neither recognized that these routines, particularly within "developed" economies, were the result of a complex of largely psychological rather than economic biases. Neither recognized that the effect of the restricted, impersonal routines fell unevenly across the relativity of human psychologies, and partly as a result of their own and their followers' omissions, the preference for the right personality continues.

The Next Level

Once again, the reasons for the continuation of these imbalances within society are not economic in and of themselves. They are a matter of the natural psychologies of different kinds of minds, for as the analytic mind draws definitional lines and thinks along these lines, a pervasively economic society casts up large institutions and gives them legitimacy by nurturing the biased transaction. Bureaucratic organizations, both private and public, order the modern state, and they encourage patterns of behavior that reflect the distribution of personalities within them. There is no such thing as "bureaucratic behavior." The behavior of structures is largely a function of the personalities that work within them, and the motivation of the lines personality, which wishes to reward individuals who identify with both the finite nature of the modern transaction and the rewards of economic achievement, is the motivation that best survives within the bureaucracy. The best evidence for this similarity is the distribution of personalities within bureaucracies; there is a clear selection of personalities within the modern organization, and that selectivity affects both the organization of the bureaucracy and the way in which bureaucracies interact with each other.

Inevitably, bureaucratic interaction becomes much like the economic transaction, and though much has been written of the "conservatism" of bureaucracies, such writing almost exclusively deals with the logical obstructions of the institution rather than with the conservative psychological qualities of bureaucracy. Little has been said of the psychologically conservative linkages that bureaucracies generate among themselves as these linkages deal with the protectiveness that is so much a part of the lines personality's attempts to insulate itself. The lines personality favors the singularity of its function and thus insures the minimum level of integration of its functioning with other bureaucracies. As with the externals of the economic transaction, the distribution of relative personalities within a large organization finds the lines personality nearer the boundaries of the structure. Psychological lines attract exterior or jurisdictional lines, and the competitive, lines personality will inevitably prefer to protect its boundaries and maintain the purity of its real or perceived jurisdiction.

Of course, selective positioning and psychologically conservative biases are not the only effect that bureaucracies generate. Along with a combative positioning of bureaucratic units toward one another, the skewed distribution of personalities within bureaucratic subunits creates a biased impact upon the specific configuration of subunits within larger bureaucracies. Again, the lines personality does not favor psychic variety; it is more comfortable with well-defined and homogeneous settings, and many social and political costs flow from this prejudice. Only the first is that the work routines within the bureaucracy tend to become highly atomized. Just as important, the very number of the bureaucratic subunits that exist within a lines personality's preferred configuration is higher than it is for those on the left of the continuum. Again, the need for psychological homogeneity within the unit is important to the lines personality, and it is just as important that the notion of "fit" at the edges is available to it. Predictably, a balkanization within bureaucracies results, and the subsequent unwillingness of any unit to risk heterogeneity and a degree of imprecision within its own jurisdictional definitions will contain both individual psychological as well as performance-related costs.

One additional by-product of the dominance of the lines personality within bureaucratic structures concerns the stability of the structural makeup of that framework. Contrary to conventional understanding, the lines or conservative personality does not prefer bureaucratic stability. Indeed, that personality is concerned with a personal defining and manipulating of the lines in a way that inevitably redefines the configurations of structures. Though this personality argues for the importance of structure, the lines personality, when it can affect jurisdictional lines within an organization, frequently readjusts those configurations and searches for personal definition within such altered structures. There is, again, a natural affinity for dealing with lines as lines even as they are revised and extended.

Finally, this preference for jurisdictional separations within a bureaucracy often reinforces, not only the tendency to alter jurisdictions, but the tendency to continue the selective placement of the lines personality along the borders of that structure as well. Such a cumulative predisposition, again, will impair the productivity of that working structure as the artificial personality configuration within the bureaucracy will impair the cooperation of one unit with the others. With the predictable intrusion of psychological bias into bureaucratic structures and the transactions among structures, imbalances of psychological equity within populations are both reinforced and magnified.

Government

We should now move to a set of considerations that go beyond either the psychological imbalances in transactions or the psychological imbalances of bureaucracy. Psychological biases bring imbalances to governmental structures as well, and, as with bureaucracy, we can examine these structures as a function of the distribution of the personalities that exist within them. To what extent, in other words, is a natural psychological balance likely to occur within governmental structures? Within each polity, a spectrum ranging from a firm allegiance to such externals as national identification or religious or social orthodoxy to lesser institutional allegiances clearly exists. To date, however, this spectrum has never been permitted to manifest itself within governmental structure. National governments do not find it in their interest to permit psychological balances; for this reason, nation-states not only support a biased concentration of economic over noneconomic valuations; they also support conservatively biased governmental structures in order to indulge their competition with other states. These imbalances are often maintained by a delicate strategy, with national regimes often subtly maintaining a prevailing economic emphasis or encouraging the development of jurisdictionally protective institutions. Such a policy surely coincides with, and indeed even promotes the "realities" of, a harsh international order. The ascendance of the lines personality and the positioning of that personality along the figurative "borders" of the modern state occur just as certainly as they do within bureaucracies.

What can we expect to find within the internal structures of governments? In governments in which the fear of external confrontation is not so great that centralization is deemed imperative, a conservative psychological bias in governmental structure is expressed in excessive structural decentralization. Two structural benchmarks of such decentralization, of course, are federalism and an institutional separation within the national jurisdictions like the American separation of powers.

Federalism is the traditional political device for concurrently providing both local and more universal sovereignty. Logically, federalism seems to contain no bias. All things equal, and within nations where the identifications of disparate peoples do not transcend the limiting boundaries of a region or that region's nationalities or languages, federalism may be a convenient device. Yet federalism within all but the most heterogeneous of states is not psychologically neutral, and understanding the range of personalities reveals how strong political identifications with the local and more homogeneous "sovereignty" will psychologically negate any larger national identification.

The lines personality, as we would expect, prefers both the homogeneity of a familiar population and the psychological "closeness" of a delimited population's boundaries. It will, all things equal, incline to the support of an excessive federalism, along with the firmness of decentralizing lines. Conversely, the porous lines personality will more naturally identify with heterogeneous commonalities among the federated units, for, once again, though federalism is neutral logically, the position for or against federalism within specific contexts is rarely neutral psychologically. Indeed, although it is a left-of-center position when it advocates something like world federalism, the need for clearer and closer lines within the immediate political identification of the nation-state is invariably the result of a psychologically conservative view.

The bias of the conservative view is just as clearly demonstrated within preferences for structures that divide levels of government into several functional units. With federalism, the impact of the conservative mind is one of identification, a matter of familiarity or fit that jealously guards the prerogatives of a comfortable homogeneity. The conservative mind also prefers an excessive institutional competitiveness among as well as within separated institutions, and the competitive function of substructures may thus be manifested within cabinet or other governmental departments. These subunits will compete within related functions, and in doing so, they attempt to enhance the identity and separation of their own arena. The full, psychologically relativistic range of opinion and public policy preference may be forced within a larger number of separated institutions, though it would be more fully represented within a smaller number of heterogeneous institutions.

Not unlike federalism or the bureaucratic configuration, a separation of public functions at a single level of authority is not psychologically neutral. The greater the opportunity for an internal sorting out of personalities within substructures, the greater the degree of separation there is between functional institutions of government.

Incredibly, within the American government, as well as within American political parties and the American electoral process, what passed as "reforms" as late as the mid-1970s were in fact centrifugal arrangements brought on by those of the logical and not the psychological left. The increased dispersion of Congressional responsibility, the increase of Congressional staff and such things as the acceleration of the number of presidential primaries and the further complication of the budgetary process, only strengthened the centrifugal forces within the American government and enhanced the conservative advantage.

Inevitably, excessive federalism or excessive separation of institutions within a single level of government, as well as the movement of policy through the transactional subsystems that both of these devices engender, favor the conservative view. Again, subjective lines are attracted to objective lines and the greater the number of lines that divide and restrict the aggregation of the polity, the greater the likelihood that conservative biases will flow from the institutions of that government. It may be, of course, that there is an informal limit to this bias; just as the concept of federalism has historically restrained a precipitous overaggregation of the polity, so too the diffusion of governmental power may well diffuse arbitrary public power within public institutions. Nonetheless, there are natural psychological equilibriums that can inform us as to how greatly federalism and the diffusion of governmental structures should divide the aggregation. Knowledge of these equilibriums should permit us to design the separations among levels of a government and among institutions at the same level in a psychologically equitable way.

The State and the World

There is, of course, one more level to the structural bias. We are, without question, at that stage of history where the nation-state's ability to perform as a competent aggregator of the world polity is in decline. Though the matter has often been cast within a utopian setting, it is reasonable now for the issue of global organization to be raised on the grounds of both the issue of national competence and the issue of psychological bias. That segment of the psychological spectrum that naturally rejects the lines of global divisions may now speak more certainly of an emerging global polity.

Fortuitously, the misunderstandings about Hegel's alleged nationalism become relevant at this point in history. If Hegel were with us today, there is no question that his notions of the ethical over the chauvinistic state would urge us to move beyond national identifications. The essence of Hegel's dialectic almost necessitates such a conclusion, and, indeed, this final political stage, the stage of a world polity, was written about by Hegelian theorists such as Bluntschli as far back as the nineteenth century. Indeed, John William Burgess, an American political theorist who was influenced by Johann Bluntschli as well as by Hegel's belief in the coming world state, has argued that such a state was foretold not only by the dialectic itself but also by Hegel's notion of the *Sittlichkeit,* or the process of enculturation of a civilized world.[1]

Of course, many leading thinkers, including Kant, have talked of peace in the world, yet Kant's notion of "eternal peace" is founded upon the placing of each country into its proper fit within the configuration of nations. "Nations," Kant believed, are "like individual men," and he urged that the separation of the states, as with the separation of individuals, is necessary because individuals are prone to "hurt each other in the state of nature." A separation, then—or a design based upon what Kant considered to be the "objective reality" of natural separation—was how Kant would cure the proclivities of the hurtful state of nature.[2]

Prince Metternich felt much the same way about "natural" separation. Metternich's cognition of the nineteenth-century states, like so many of his contemporary and modern-day disciples, was singularly configurational, edges fitting with edges in a daily redressing of a grand equilibrium. Globally, the equilibrium of externals is still a design of separation, and when the external balances are all that we rely on, particularly when the relative power and the configurational "fit" of the nation-states is nearly always in fluctuation, there is little chance for international equilibrium.

Without question, however, the passage of time will bring equity to the Natural Left. Not only has history demonstrated the resilience of centripetal forces, with nearly 5 billion people now within the borders of 165 states, but the recognition of the psychological range and the natural emergence of those considerations which would naturally be raised by those of a more conscious psychological identification will expose the psychological bias of the national subdivision as the national subunit increasingly interacts in much the same way as economic units or balkanized bureaucracies or national governments do. How much government should there be at a global level? The standard is not difficult: there should be no less government than what the natural business of the world society suggests, that being the standard for any other government. There is no date or prescribed avenue for global political reconciliation, but for those who choose not to recognize the ascendancy of the global union, let the recent history of economic integration stand as the best evidence of the world right's quiet commitment to it. The Natural Left may now justly ask for what amounts to an agenda of *equivalent ascendance* in return.

For unrestricted global capital and investment, we ask for unrestricted global education of increasing numbers of the ensuing generations. For markets and the earth's materials, we ask for the ascendance of political linkages such as a union of interests and even, political parties. To those who ask for arrangements that insure the stability of their worldly transactions, we now may ask for those things which redress the inequities of transactions at the global level as well. Finally, to those who fear a single world order and the decline of national assurances against abuses that would arise from that order, let it be clear that such anticipatory fear is balanced by the imbalances which the world right has already brought us. In short, though the relativist view recognizes no exclusive claim upon political arrangements, it has the right to redress the imbalance that has occurred since World War II. It has the right to equivalent ascendance.

The Emerging Philosophy

Of course, over the long run, the redress of imbalance will be assisted by the emerging political philosophy. Though the "verticals" or objective factors will inevitably retain their importance, the preoccupation with these variables is more clearly than ever at an end. The essence of a conscious and relativistic subjectivism will not only enrich political philosophy but will aid in the generation of the institutional equivalences in the real world as well.

Even today, the logical left finds itself concerned with such questions as the North/South dichotomy, a concern that grows out of a genuine and proper identification with economically disadvantaged areas of the world. Yet what did logically left movements create at the national level when they relied upon economic theory to redress the North-South imbalance? Predictably, they only institutionalized the sanctity of economics, while they pruned what little of the Natural Left there was that might have lived within their appeal. Now this time at a global level, the logical left threatens to restrict the argument again and thus impose the burden of economism on the world as well as on the lesser developed countries.

Of course, the greatest ally that the economic interests possess in the extension of the imbalances of economism is the nation-state itself. The checkerboard of national subpolities has provided the world right with its choice among the "sovereignties" in its fostering of economic interests and more importantly the very transactions within the World Right that exist among the psychologies that protect the nation-state affirm the psychological importance of that state to the right's ascendance. Though it is tempting, the argument concerning national sovereignty must never be made solely with respect to the imbalances within a single transaction or bureaucracy or even with respect to the internal loyalty to a state. These imbalances are very much a part of what, at least within the alliance of the multinationals and the grand commercial states, is a clear attempt at maintaining the ideological alliance of the right. They, the right, very much want the argument kept at that level. Of course, the lesser figures of the right, the national presidents and prime ministers, have been assigned the task of parading themselves at that lower level; what the independent actors of the right want most is to never have the discussion ascend to what would fairly identify them for what they are. Postponing the time when the world becomes the salient polity is paramount for them, because they understand that a constituted world citizenry will require a different standard for both economism and psychological balance.

History, however, will continue to move beyond the nation-state, though that movement will not by itself guarantee political equity if the Natural Left does not create a political philosophy that speaks to the world polity as well as to psychological equity. If the arguments over economic distribution are isolated from the larger framework, the more significant challenges concerning the restoration of a psychological equilibrium will simply lose themselves among global economism. There is one misunderstanding that the emerging Natural Left must never have. Once and for all, the left should persuade itself that no nation-state or bloc of nation states represents their interest. Neither the "proper" resolution of the current conflict between contemporary states nor the accession of ostensibly left-wing states in the world order will insure psychological equity. The harsh fact is that there are no left-wing states, for the institution of the nation-state itself and the internal and external psychological

AN EMERGING PHILOSOPHY OF POLITICS

imbalances that the nation-states as a group have caused will never permit the true left to flower. Subjective lines find objective lines again, and the same protective psychologies that border the bureaucratic and internally balkanized powers of a government make up the protective walls of nations.

As we progress through an interpretation of the individual transaction through the biases of bureaucratic structure and the functional units of the nation-state, the configurations of lines against lines at the level of the state act as a reinforcer for the psychological imbalances back through the progression. Perhaps, as it becomes apparent that the biases are linked among these levels, it will become apparent that the very existence of the nation-state contributes to the accented influence of the lines personality at the border of each descendant institution or interaction. The solution for the Natural Left can never be a matter of solving one level's problems. We must plan for the larger balances at the outset, and though there can be no single stratagem, the Natural Left must always be comprehensive, even exhaustive, in its proposals.

Let us also not forget that the position of the Natural Left specifically offers relativism, and by doing so, it specifically extends a promise of equity to the psychological right. In return, it insists upon the inclusion of Aristotle's third level, or the aggregated reason of the relativistic subjective view. The success of the Natural Left will depend upon its asking for what is its own within an understanding of the just claims of the right. If the great division within metaethics is now psychological rather than logical, and if the conservative portion of the metaethical division and its disciplinary progeny have maintained a dominance over the Natural Left, it is time for those who are of the Natural Left to collect their philosophy around them and confront the advantaged side. To date, the conflicts of the world have prevented the acceptance of human relativism at the same time that economically dominated political philosophy has held its singular view of human nature. The philosophies that nation-states believe in (and seem so ready to fight for) are in great part the archaic remains of outdated intellectual understandings. We will be nearer the transcendence of that conflict when we offer a political philosophy based upon a true relativism.

Of course, the psychological right is justified in arguing for the natural hierarchies within the human population; the denial of their existence is a false position for relativism. Mill was not in error in speaking of the "higher qualities," and there are natural places for largely contigual arrangements in the affairs of humankind as well. Also, respect for superior skill and the wisdom of age, and for the universality of certain social institutions, are not only proper identifications but also necessary strands in the warp and woof of any society. Indeed, denying the right's contribution to the aggregated reason in the dissembling of such orders would visit many of the same difficulties upon us that the excesses of overorder have brought in the past.

What the Natural Left must emphasize is that there are natural horizontals that make up the linkages of society as well. Surely, the family can and should remain as a place of deep affection as well as an instrument of mere stability. The confluence of both associative and functionally shared tasks must exist within their natural settings, and economic achievement must no longer carry the price of psychological imbalance. The awesome calculus of violence, child abuse, alcoholism, use of drugs, divorce, and suicide along with the decline of personal serenity among so many affluent people must continue to remind us of the link between psychological and political imbalances. Unfortunately, the very argument for a complementary view of humankind is impeded by teachings and writings that are themselves the result of balkanized and biased disciplines. Thus, as the Natural Left asks for a full agenda for the world, so too it must ask for a full agenda within the disciplines, a step that will not likely be taken without a broad acceptance of intellectual relativism. That relativism is at the core of both the political and the intellectual argument is now more clear than at any time since Hegel, for without question, the *Bildung,* or the evolving understanding that the emerging philosophy requires, accompanies the emergence of the relativist/rationalist coalition on the left that Hegel initiated. Without question, only a full flowering of that coalition will precede the flowering of the Natural Left.

In closing, I am reminded of Antoine Lavoisier, the founder of modern chemistry, whose central contribution was his notion that the quantity of matter is constant and that what is used up or altered in some manner is still very much with us. That is how it has been in political philosophy, for in our nonrelativistic attempts at divining the human equilibrium, the very factors that we did not consider were the components of the overflow or residuum of the incomplete theory. The residue of the unequal transactional exchange, of the artificial incentives to economism or the artificially structured bureaucracies, accompanied by the imbalances of politics, has been tucked away within the residuum of psychology. In the real world, they have exacted their price largely at one end of the psychological continuum, and, without an acceptance of the primacy of that very continuum, they will remain there.

Let me repeat in closing what I suggested earlier. The Natural Left is the only true left. The turning of the axis of the political dialogue, foretold by the rotation of the metaethical axis, has proceeded from the considerations of purely economic contribution to the considerations of relative value and complementary contribution. As a result of this rotation, the political Left will increasingly ask for political equity within the context of what its mind and psyche naturally create. The Natural Left will inevitably expand the very breadth of the dialogue, and, for those who understand only a singular psychology, the lessons of the emerging philosophy as well as what remains for Hegelian metaphysical relativism will be lost. For those who understand the relativity that the Natural Left brings, the rainbow of the aggregate reason will decorate their world.

NOTES

1. Daniel R. Sabia, "A Historiography of Political Theory," Ph.D. diss., University of Minnesota, 1978.
2. Immanuel Kant, "To Eternal Peace," in Carl J. Friedrich, ed., *The Philosophy of Kant* (New York: Modern Library, 1949), p. 44.

Index

"Academic Sociology," 124
Adam, Smith
   and natural value, 15
Adorno, T. W.
   The Authoritarian Personality, 49, 50, 52, 153
Adriaansens, Hans, 123
Alienation, 155
Analytics
   and the law, 100
Anarchism, 151
Anthropology, 32
Aquinas, Thomas, 93, 103
Aristotle, 11, 12, 19, 34, 42, 57, 58, 79, 143, 158, 162
   and reason, 3
   Politics, 1, 2
Aron, Raymond, 152
Atomism, 147
Augustine, 12
Austin, John, 91, 94, 95, 96, 101, 108

Bachofen, J. J., 130, 131, 134
Barker, Ernest, 88
Bastian, Adolphe, 130, 131, 134
Bazard, Saint-Armand, 124
Behaviorism
   Skinnerian, 125
Below, Von Georg, 118
Benedict, Ruth, 32, 33, 40, 128, 133
Bentham, Jeremy, 85, 91, 94, 107, 108, 109, 112

Benthamite radicals, 146
Berger, Peter, 75
Berger, Victor, 148
Berlin, Isaiah, 6, 11, 53
Bernstein, Eduard, 152
Bernstein, Richard, 10
   The Restructuring of Social and Political Theory, 6
Bildung, 36
Blackstone, William, 85-88*passim*, 94, 95, 98, 106, 109
Blakeslee, Thomas, 53
Blanc, Louis, 151
Blanqui, Auguste, 111, 151
Bloomfield, Leonard, 133
Bluntschli, Johann, 170
Boas, Franz, 129, 131, 132, 133
Boorstin, Daniel, 93
   The Mysterious Science of the Law, 87
Brecht, Arnold, 31, 32, 33, 34, 51, 75
   and "biographical and biological differences," 39, 78
Brown, Richard, H., 126, 127
Brown, Roger, 50
Buchanan, James, 116
Bureaucracy
   stability, 166
Bureaucratic behavior, 165
Burgess, John William, 170

Cahnman, Werner, 118, 119
Calhoun, John C., 146

178 INDEX

Camus, Albert, 152
Carnap, Rudolf, 132
Chomsky, Noam, 133
  and deep structure, 10
Christian orthodoxy, 12
Cicero, 27
Cochrane, James, 113
Coke, Edward, 84
Common law, 84, 86, 94, 107
Comte, Auguste, 72, 73, 74, 84, 118, 119, 124
Confederacy, American, 146
Construct variables, 50
Copernicus, Nicholai, 12
Cowan, Thomas, 78
Cumming, Robert, 108

Dahrendorf, Ralf, 120, 121, 122
Darlington, C. D., 51, 52
Darwinism, 72
Debs, Eugene, 148
d'Entreves, A. P., 90, 92, 93
Descartes, René, 13, 28, 68, 71, 72, 129
de Sismondi, 110
Devlin, Lord, 97
Dualism and monism, 129, 131
Duguit, Léon, 98, 99
Duns Scotus, 12
Du Pont, Pierre Samuel, 106
Durkheim, Emile, 117, 119, 120, 125, 132
Dworkin, Ronald, 104, 105

Economics
  classical school of, 106, 111
Einstein, Albert, 29, 31, 76, 77
Ekeh, Peter, 117
Enclosures, 107
Enfantin, Barthélemy, 124
Engels, Friedrich, 152
Enlightenment, 12, 13, 14, 16, 25, 37
Epicureans, 27
Ethnomethodology, 11
Existentialism, 157
Eysenck, Hans, 59
  and "cortical stimulus equilibriums," 52, 57

Fabians, 149, 150, 151
Fascism, 152
Fechner, Gustav, 132
Federalism, 167-68
Feuerback, Ludwig, 156
Feyerabend, Paul, 115
Findlay, J. W., 39, 43, 65, 66, 67
Fisher, Kuno, 37
Fourier, Charles, 110, 150
Frankfurt school, 9
  and critical school, 11
Frederick the Great, 86
Frederick William IV, 118
French Revolution, 13, 29, 144, 146, 150
Freud, Sigmund, 10, 11, 51
Friedman, Milton, 115
Friedrich, Carl, 20, 21, 37, 39, 40
Fromm, Erich, 158
F-scale, 50
Fuller, Lon, 100, 101, 102, 103, 105
Functionalism, 98, 99
Fusfeld, Daniel, 115
  and psychological foundations, 117

Galileo, 12, 13
Garfinkel, Harold, 11
Gény, Francois, 102, 103
Gestalt psychology, 134
Giddens, Anthony, 118
Gierke, Otto Von, 100
  and natural law, 88
Godwin, William, 149
Gombin, Richard, 153
  Les Origins du Gauchisme, 152
Gouldner, Alvin, 117, 125, 126
  The Coming Crisis of Western Sociology, 124
Governmental structure, 167
Grotius, Hugo, 83, 84, 93
Grundnorm, 95

Habermas, Jürgen, 39
  and cognitive interests, 9
  and general structures, 10
Harding, Arthur, 102, 103
Harris, Marvin
  The Rise of Anthopological Theory, 131
Harrod, Ray, 113

# INDEX

Hart, H. L. A., 96, 97, 100, 101, 102, 105, 122
Hayden, Tom, 148
Hayek, Friedrich von, 116
Hegel, G. W. F., 9, 17, 28, 35-44*passim*, 51, 54, 62, 65, 68, 70, 76, 77, 79, 89, 90, 93, 101, 103, 119, 124, 127, 130, 131, 133, 144, 156, 158, 169, 170, 174
  and causation, 6
  and epistemology, 38
  and idealism, 157
  and relativism, 67, 75
Herder, Johann, 130
Herskovits, Melville, 33
Hess, Moses, 151
Hicks, John R., 113
Hildebrand, Bruno, 88, 111
Historical school, 119
  legal, 88
Historicism, 87, 89, 119
  economic, 88, 107, 111
  German, 98, 118
  legal, 90, 93, 94, 99, 106, 111
Hobbes, Thomas, 91, 95, 96, 100, 108, 121
Hollitscher, Walter, 29, 31, 76
Holmes, Oliver Wendell, 100
Homans, George, 125
Hooker, Richard, 15, 83, 84, 85, 93
Horizontalism, 2, 79, 164
Horkheimer, Max, 153
Hull, Clark L., 132
Human equity, 3
Hume, David, 14, 18, 20, 22, 23, 71, 85, 107, 112, 114
  and epistemology, 17
  and general theories, 17
  A Treatise of Human Nature, 16
Husserl, Edmund, 7, 8
Hyppolite, Jean, 35, 40

Imperative school of law, 92
Industrialism, 76
Industrialization, 14

Jacobins, 29
James, William, 147
Jefferson, Thomas, 15, 146
Jevons, William, 112, 131
Jung, Carl, 54
Junkers, 118
Justinian, 27

Kant, Immanuel, 14, 18, 19, 20, 23, 24, 28, 32, 33, 35, 37, 38, 40, 43, 44, 62, 63, 64, 65, 68-71*passim*, 77, 90-94*passim*, 104, 127, 130, 170
  and fear of relativism, 25
  and reality and norms, 21
  and synthetic knowledge, 20, 21
  and the Categorical Imperative, 10, 74
  "Dreams of a Visionary," 22, 26
  "Prolegomena," 25
Kantianism, 14
Kaufman, Walter, 71
Kelsen, Hans, 95, 96, 100, 101
Keynes, John Meynard, 112, 113, 114
Keynesianism, 115
Kierkegaard, Sören, 157
Knies, Karl, 88, 111
Kocourek, Robert, 91
Korsch, Karl, 153
Kreml, W. P.
  The Anti-Authoritarian Personality, 50, 55
Krupp, Sherman
  and new variables, 116
Kuhn, Thomas, 117
Kuper, Adam, 132

Lassalle, Ferdinand, 151
Lavoisier, Antoine, 174
Leaf, Murray, 130, 132, 133, 134
  Man, Mind and Science, 129
Lebenswelt, 7, 8
Left
  and history, 144
  continental, 150
  logical, 150, 152, 161, 162, 168
  modern, 152
  psychological, 62, 150, 152, 168
  utopian, 149
  see also New Left
Leibniz, G. W., 20
Lenin, V. I., 146, 153

Lettrists, 153
Lévi-Bruhl, Lucien, 132
Lévi-Straus, Claude, 117, 129, 133
Locke, John, 15, 84, 85, 91, 92, 99, 107, 147
   An Essay Concerning Human Understanding, 15
Logic, 43
Logical left *See* Left
Loubser, Jan, 129
Loye, David, 41
Lukac, George, 153

MacDonald, Ramsay, 152
McKenzie, Richard, 114, 115
Madison, James, 146, 147
Maine, Henry, 107
Malinowski, Bronislaw, 129, 132
Malthus, Thomas, 112, 156
Marcuse, Herbert, 158
Marginal utility, 112
Marshall, Alfred, 112, 113
Meek, Richard, 113
Marx, Karl, 9, 111, 118, 124, 125, 152-56*passim*, 164
   Critique of the Gotha Programme, 154
   materialism, 156, 157
   The Economical and Political Manuscripts, 154
Marxism, 9, 122, 123, 151, 152, 157
Marxists, 158
Maslow, Abraham, 41
Mayer, Thomas, 114
Mayrl, William, 11
Mead, Margaret, 32, 133
Meek, Richard, 113
Menger, Karl, 112, 119
Mercantilism, 110
Merleau-Ponty, Maurice, 134, 152
   Les Aventures de la Dialectique, 153
Merton, Robert, 121, 123
méson, 1, 99
Metaethical division, 28, 29, 30, 42, 49, 66, 68, 73, 78, 79, 91, 105, 113, 124, 143, 144, 157, 174, 175
   and sociology, 119
   in the law, 95
Metaethical school, 43
Metaphysics, 13

Metternich, Fürst von, 170
Mill, John Stuart, 109, 110, 112, 113, 173
   The Principles of Political Economy, 108
Mind-body dichotomy, 9
Mitroff, Ian, 53, 60, 78, 155
Montesquieu, C. L., 26, 33, 34, 35, 38, 54, 129, 157
Morgan, Lewis, 134
Myrdal, Gunnar, 116

Nabors, Lawrence, 116
Nagel, Ernest, 6
Nationalism, 78
National sovereignty, 172
Nation-state, 169, 170
Natural law, 83, 85, 86, 87, 88, 90-100*passim*, 102, 103, 107, 110
   and Blackstone, 94
Natural right, 15, 83, 84, 85
Neo-Kantianism, 40, 95, 119
Neurath, Otto, 131
New Left, 124, 126
Newton, Isaac, 78
   Principia, 12
Nietzsche, Friedrich, 24, 70, 71, 74, 95
Nihilism, 27
Nihilists, 73
Nozick, Robert, 115

Østerberg, Dag, 127, 128
Owen, Robert, 110, 149

Paine, Thomas, 146
Panneloeck, Anton, 153
Paris Commune, 151
Parsons, Talcott, 117, 121, 122, 123, 124, 125
Phenomenology, 6, 7, 11, 35, 38
Physiocrats, 105, 106
Planck, Max, 76
Plato, 5, 27
Platonists, 27
Political theory, 144
Popper, Karl, 126
Positivism, 6, 7, 14, 72, 73, 75, 101, 115, 118, 121, 125, 127, 128
   and the law, 83
   Spencerian, 125
Positivists, 6, 71

INDEX

Pound, Roscoe, 88, 98, 99
Process
   analytic, 53, 66
   synthetic, 53
Prognosticism, 147
Protagoras, 27
Proudhon, Pierre, 151
Psychological Left *See* Left
Puchta, G. F., 89
Pufendorf, Samuel von, 34, 83, 84, 85, 92

Quesnay, Francois, 106

Radcliffe-Brown, A. R., 132, 133
Rationalism, 13, 18
Rawls, John, 104
Reason, 4, 11-16*passim,* 18, 20, 21, 23, 24, 26, 28, 30, 32, 33, 35, 37, 39, 41-44*passim,* 49, 58, 64, 65, 67, 70, 77, 79, 86, 87, 88, 90, 95, 100, 103, 104, 143, 155
   aggregate, 43, 173, 175
   See also Aristotle
Reformation, 12
Reign of Terror, 29
Relativity, 30
Renaissance, 28
Ricardo, David, 106, 108, 112, 113, 156
Robespierre, Maximilien, 146
Robinson, Joan, 114
Rokeach, Milton
   The Open and Closed Mind, 50
Roll, Eric, 110, 115
Romanticism, 78, 87, 110, 118, 119
   German, 90
Rommen, Heinrich, 91
Roscher, Wilhelm, 111
Rothenberg, Jerome, 116, 117
Rousseau, Jean Jacques, 14, 25, 118, 121
Russian Revolution, 146

Saint-Simon, Henri de, 72, 110, 124, 150, 151
Samuelson, Paul, 115
Sartre, Jean-Paul, 152
Savigny, Frederick von, 88, 89, 90
Say, Jean Baptiste, 110
Say's law, 106

Schackle, G. L. S., 116
Schapper, Karl, 151
Schelling, Thomas C., 131
Schmoller, Gustav von, 119
Schopenhauer, Arthur, 24, 40, 69, 70, 74, 95
Schumpeter, Joseph, 112
Schutz, Alfred, 8, 39
Scott-Craig, Thomas S. K., 91
Sellars, Wilfrid, 7
Separation of powers, 167
Sextus, Empiricus, 13
Silk, Leonard, 116
Simmel, George, 117, 119
Simonde, Jean Charles, 110
Situationists, 153
Skepticism, 14, 18, 20, 23, 24, 27, 28, 33, 38, 41, 42, 71, 73, 75, 98, 107, 110, 114, 118, 119, 128, 130, 131, 143
   random, 29, 30, 31, 32
   relativist, 29, 30
Skinner, B. F., 132
Smelser, Neil, 126
Smith, Adam, 87, 112, 164
   natural value, 106
Social Democrats, 149
Socialism, 110, 111
Socrates, 27
Sophists, 27, 66, 121
Sophocles, 91
Spencer, Herbert, 72, 73, 74, 98, 119, 120, 147
Sraffa, Pierro, 114
Stammler, Rudolph, 89
Stoics, 27
Structural functionalism, 122
Structural reform, 168
Stylistic variables, 50

Tawney, R. H., 149
Technocracy, 150
Thomas, Norman, 148
Thrasymachus, 27, 121, 122
Tocqueville, Alexis de, 118
Turgot, Anne Robert Jacques, 106
Turner, Victor, 134
Twain, Mark, 148
Tylor, E. B., 131

United States Constitution, 15, 146
  Civil War Amendments, 147
Utilitarianism, 14, 17, 85, 123
  and the law, 83
  economic, 106
  legal, 94
Utilitarians, 16
Utopianism, 151

Verticalism, 2, 49, 154, 155, 157
Vienna circle, 131
Voltaire, 14, 85-88*passim,* 94, 98, 106

Walrus, Léon, 112
Wasserstrom, Richard, 105, 117
Weber, Max, 117, 118, 119
  Economics and Security, 119
Weintraub, Sidney, 114
Western philosophy, 5, 11
Western thought, 40
Whitman, Walt, 148
Whorf, Benjamin Lee, 134
Wilson, Harold, 149
Witling, William, 151
Wittgenstein, Ludwig, 72
Wundt, William, 134